Cornerstones of Strong Schools

Practices for Purposeful Leadership

Jeffrey Zoul
Laura Link

EYE ON EDUCATION
6 DEPOT WAY WEST, SUITE 106
LARCHMONT, NY 10538
(914) 833–0551
(914) 833–0761 fax
www.eyeoneducation.com

Library of Congress Cataloging-in-Publication Data

Zoul, Jeffrey.
Cornerstones of strong schools : practices for purposeful leadership / Jeffrey
Zoul, Laura Link.
     p. cm.
  Includes bibliographical references.
  ISBN-13: 978-1-59667-068-6
1. Educational leadership—United States. 2. School management and organi-
zation—United States. I. Link, Laura. II. Title.
  LB2805.Z678 2007
  371.2—dc22

                      2007031557

10 9 8 7 6 5 4 3 2 1

Also Available from EYE ON EDUCATION

Improving Your School One Week At a Time:
Building the Foundation for Professional Teaching & Learning
Jeffrey Zoul

What Great Principals Do Differently:
15 Things That Matter Most
Todd Whitaker

The Principal as Instructional Leader:
A Handbook for Supervisors, Second Edition
Sally J. Zepeda

What Successful Principals Do!
169 Tips for Principals
Franzy Fleck

Lead With Me:
A Principal's Guide to Teacher Leadership
Gayle Moller and Anita Pankake

The Instructional Leader's
Guide to Informal Classroom Observations
Sally J. Zepeda

Lead Me – I Dare You!
Sherrel Bergman and Judith Brough

From At-Risk to Academic Excellence:
What Successful Leaders Do
Schargel, Thacker and Bell

Countdown to the Principalship:
A Resource Guide for Beginning Principals
O'Rourke, Provenzano, Bellamy, and Ballek

The Principal's Purpose:

A Practical Guide to Moral and Ethical Leadership
Leanna Stohr Isaacson

Smart, Fast, Efficient:
The New Principals' Guide to Success
Leanna Stohr Isaacson

Creating the High Schools of Our Choice
Tim Westerberg

BRAVO Principal!
Sandra Harris

**The Administrator's Guide
to School Community Relations, Second Edition**
George E. Pawlas

**School Leader Internship: Developing, Monitoring,
and Evaluating Your Leadership Experience, 2nd Ed.**
Martin, Wright, Danzig, Flanary, and Brown

**Talk It Out!
The Educator's Guide to Successful Difficult Conversations**
Barbara E. Sanderson

**Making the Right Decisions:
A Guide for School Leaders**
Douglas J. Fiore and Chip Joseph

Dealing with Difficult Teachers, Second Edition
Todd Whitaker

**Dealing with Difficult Parents
(And with Parents in Difficult Situations)**
Todd Whitaker and Douglas Fiore

20 Strategies for Collaborative School Leaders
Jane Clark Lindle

Great Quotes for Great Educators
Todd Whitaker and Dale Lumpa

**Elevating Student Voice:
How to Enhance Participation, Citizenship, & Leadership**
Nelson Beaudoin

**Stepping Outside Your Comfort Zone:
Lessons for School Leaders**
Nelson Beaudoin

**What Great Teachers Do Differently:
14 Things That Matter Most**
Todd Whitaker

Data Analysis for Continuous School Improvement
Victoria L. Bernhardt

Dedication

To my father, Robert Zoul, who served as the primary cornerstone in my life for eighty years and to my daughter, Jordyn Zoul, who fills that role today.

Jeff Zoul

To my children: Natalie and Nolan. In you, I see the humor, grace, compassion, and courage essential to becoming effective and inspirational leaders of tomorrow.

Laura Link

About the Authors

Dr. Jeff Zoul is a principal with the Forsyth County School System in Cumming, Georgia. Prior to becoming principal at Otwell Middle School, Dr. Zoul served as a teacher, coach, and assistant principal at the elementary, middle, and high school levels for 20 years. In addition, Dr. Zoul serves as an adjunct professor of graduate studies at North Georgia College and State University. He is the author of *Improving Your School One Week at a Time: Building the Foundation for Professional Teaching and Learning* and coauthor of *Study Guide: What Great Principals Do Differently: 15 Things that Matter Most.* Dr. Zoul has presented at national conferences on a wide variety of educational issues. He earned his doctoral degree from the University of Alabama and holds additional degrees from the University of Massachusetts at Amherst, Troy State University, and the University of Southern Mississippi. Please contact Jeff at jzoul@eyeonedcation.com.

Ms. Laura Link serves as an assistant principal at Otwell Middle School in Forsyth County, Georgia. The majority of her professional experience has been at the high school level, where she has served as assistant principal and was selected as Teacher of the Year for her school as well as the entire school system. Her professional career includes 13 years of teaching service at the elementary, middle, high, and college levels. Ms. Link is National-Board certified, is Teacher Support Specialist certified, and holds two degrees from Florida State University and North Georgia College and State University. Ms. Link is recognized as an accomplished presenter in the areas of professional learning, teacher collaboration, and improving student and teacher learning. Please contact Laura at llink@eyeoneducation.com.

If you would like information about inviting the authors to speak to your group, please contact Jeff Zoul at jeffzoul@comcast.net or 770-887-8134; Laura Link can be reached at llink@forsyth.k12.ga.us or 678-939-9331.

Table of Contents

1

Crafting a Community of Leaders and Learners

Today many school leaders are charged with creating exemplary schools in which all school community members focus on learning, rather than teaching, as their fundamental business. In such schools, establishing and maintaining a culture in which the norm of *adequate* learning as well as meeting *minimum* standards and *reasonable* expectations gives way to a new vision of what we can and must become. This vision views learning for all as the school's primary focus and reason for existing. Such learning must be monitored, measured, and analyzed. We must craft learning communities focused on results. To accomplish all this, we need strong leadership, particularly at the school level. Building principals of kindergarten through grade 12 (K–12) are the primary leaders within their school community and are the determining variable as to whether their schools move from merely good, as Collins (2001) suggests, to great.

To become truly exceptional, rather than merely adequate, schools must focus on learning in a purposeful manner. That is, school leaders must plan with a highly focused purpose, and that purpose must be to improve levels of learning for all students. A purposeful learning community has been defined as having "the collective efficacy and capacity to develop and use assets to accomplish goals that matter to all community members through agreed-upon processes" (Marzano, Waters, & McNulty, 2005, p. 99). Others have written about similar communities using slightly different terminology. Schlechty (2005) writes of *learning communities, communities of learners*, and *learning organizations*. Using Schlechty's definitions, learning organizations most closely parallel the previously defined purposeful learning community. In his model learning organizations are characterized by diffuse power structures, authority based on consent and consensus, disciplined and informed decision making, an emphasis on contributing to group learning, and an inclusive membership based on one's ability to contribute to the life of the organization.

Serving as a precursor, perhaps, to the terms *purposeful learning communities* and *learning organizations* defined above, the concept of "professional learning communities" was introduced by DuFour and Eaker (1998). The authors painstakingly focused on and defined all three words of this concept, stressing that *professionals* have expertise and must remain current in the evolving knowledge base of their field. *Learning* was defined as acting in an ongoing way and with perpetual curiosity. *Community* referred to a group which is bonded by interests commonly held.

Beginning with the idea of professional learning communities and moving beyond to the ideas of purposeful learning communities and learning organizations, educational scholars, researchers, and theorists realized the need for strong school leadership that would positively affect school results. The preceding-referenced scholars all recognize the need for strong school leadership on the part of both teachers and administrators. Each envisions schools characterized both by collaborative, inclusive *learning* as well as by collaborative, inclusive *leadership* with all school community members working together for a common purpose. Although most educational leaders realize that student demographic variables have an effect on results, the best ones also realize that the actions we take as school leaders are equally important variables. Our actions as leaders may even be of greater importance than student variables. Focusing on learning and leadership, Reeves calls for "learning leaders" who believe in and are committed to the idea that "adult variables, including the professional practices of teachers and the decisions leaders make, can be more important than demographic variables" (2006, p. xxiii). In this book, we acknowledge the need for teachers to serve as leaders and that the professional practices in which they engage have a direct relationship with student learning. But the primary focus of this work is to identify and examine what it is that school administrators can and should do to improve school, teacher, and student performance.

We maintain that a "knowing-doing gap" (Pfeffer & Sutton, 2000) exists in nearly all areas of education, which prevents us from realizing dramatic school improvement on a wide-scale basis. That is, we often *know* what works, yet we fail to *do* anything within our own schools to ensure that change for the better becomes deeply embedded and widely practiced. This is true in terms of classroom instruction as well as school leadership. This book is an effort to close this gap between knowing what should be done in terms of school leadership and actually doing those things in a consistent and systematic manner. Much of what has been researched in the area of educational leadership and its effect on student achievement since 1970 has been thoroughly examined and expertly synthesized through the rigorous meta-analysis conducted by Marzano and colleagues (2005) in *School Leadership that Works: From Research to Results*. In this volume the authors identified 21 leadership responsibilities that have a significant effect on student achievement. Of these 21 leadership responsibilities, the authors suggest that 9 must be addressed by the school principal to craft a purposeful learning community:

1. Optimizer
2. Affirmation
3. Ideals/beliefs
4. Situational awareness
5. Visibility
6. Relationships
7. Communication
8. Culture
9. Input

In an earlier work, Zoul wrote about building the foundation for professional teaching and learning (2006a). That book offered ways that administrators and principals can work together to share the daunting leadership load which we all face at the K–12 level. Marzano and colleagues also recognize the importance of understanding that school leadership is not the domain of any single person; instead, the school principal must enlist the support of a team of individual school leaders. In fact, the first step in the authors' five-step plan for helping school leaders improve student achievement is to develop a strong leadership team (2005). We concur wholeheartedly. Principals must not only establish such leadership teams but sincerely value each individual team member by actively listening and engaging them only in the important work related to teaching and learning as opposed to mundane operational matters.

Although nearly all principals agree that no single individual can lead a school effectively, many would support the findings that certain areas of school leadership should remain the primary responsibility of the principal. We believe that the nine leadership responsibilities previously listed are the foundation, or cornerstones, of effective principal leadership. Planning for these nine areas of responsibility and examining how principals have and can incorporate these responsibilities into their everyday leadership behavior are essential practices for principals who want to make a difference in terms of student achievement.

As principals we are increasingly focused on the results we produce through our efforts as school leaders. We contend that this book provides concrete strategies for improving leadership practices that, carried out consistently, make a positive difference in those results. Perhaps no educational scholar has focused more on results than Mike Schmoker, who calls isolation the "enemy of improvement" (2006, p. 23). Although he highlights the deleterious influence of isolation within education in his book *Results Now*, Schmoker primarily maligns the problem of teacher isolation rather than principal isolation. In recent years, administrators have worked hard to encourage teacher collaboration in an effort to improve student achievement. Yet, too often, administrators fail to collaborate among themselves or collaborate directly with teachers in their learning communities to identify, examine, and address school improvement issues. To be sure, teachers have a more direct and immediate affect on student learning than principals. Some (Whitaker, 2003) have gone as far as suggesting that ultimately, the only two viable ways to improve a school are by hiring better teachers or improving those already in place. However, if we agree that instruction (primarily the domain of teachers) has the most prominent affect on student learning, should we not also agree that principals must be fully aware of what is occurring in classrooms where this instruction (and hopefully learning) is occurring?

Elmore (2000) suggests that schools are protected by a buffer, which encourages teacher and administrator isolation and discourages close scrutiny of teaching and learning practices. Schmoker (2006) agrees that such a buffer exists, which ensures that "building principals know very little about what teachers teach, or how well they teach" (p. 13). This practice runs counter to the leadership responsibility that Marzano and colleagues call "situational awareness" (2005). Principals must ensure that such buffers are destroyed so that they are intimately knowledgeable about what and how well teachers teach. Doing so, of course, means breaking down long-standing barriers. The concept of professional learning communities must extend beyond classroom teachers to include school administrators. As administrators, we must become more aware of our data and annual performance as well as our daily instructional practices in each and every classroom within our schools.

Not surprisingly, our task is rife with challenges and obstacles. It requires a paradigm shift as well as a great deal of work. Marzano and colleagues speak of "school leadership that *works*" (2005). We suggest that two distinct definitions of the italicized term apply. Although the research they uncovered clearly works (in the sense that applying their findings proves *effective*) for principals, we cannot escape the fact that, even with their action plan for making the process as efficient as possible, much work (*effort*) is required on the part of principals and all school leaders. When faced with any seemingly daunting undertaking at our own school, we often invoke the widely known adage, "Few burdens are heavy if everyone lifts." There are times, we confess, when we suspect that school leadership is an exception to this typically uplifting rule. Even with the support of an administrative team and expert teacher leaders, the principal's responsibilities are wide ranging, challenging, stressful, and require long hours on the job. Although there is no getting around the fact that the work facing principals is increasingly demanding, it is also true that it is possible to work smarter, rather than merely harder.

The key to working smarter is to work with a *purpose,* which brings us back to the idea of crafting purposeful learning communities within our schools. Our work must be relevant to the results we aim to achieve. What follows is an effort to make that connection between relevance and results. Our work must be highly focused and efficiently carried out. Although a thriving purposeful learning community is where a strong leadership team is developed, maintained, and actively involved in fulfilling many of the 21 leadership responsibilities, such a community must originate with the leadership decisions and actions of the principal (Marzano, et al., 2005). These decisions and actions, which are precursors to crafting, nurturing, and cultivating a purposeful learning community, can be aligned with the nine aforementioned principal responsibilities. Principals must effectively execute these nine responsibilities while inviting other school leaders to join in this leadership journey along the way.

The following chapters include insights into each leadership responsibility along with practical, specific strategies to purposefully execute them. These responsibilities are the cornerstones on which purposeful learning communities are built, schools focused on targeting goals and achieving intended results. A *cornerstone* can be defined as "an indispensable and fundamental basis" and "the fundamental assumptions from which something is begun or developed" (American Heritage, 2000). Considered literally, a cornerstone is often marked and placed in a prominent exterior wall position of a public building, marking the building's origin. Figuratively speaking, the nine leadership responsibilities of school principals, necessary for building a purposeful learning community, serve as cornerstones of another kind. As the dictionary definition suggests, they serve as the "indispensable" and "fundamental" basis for successful school leadership from which something of vital importance is "begun" or "developed." That "something of vital importance" is the academic achievement of millions of young people attending our nation's schools.

Each day when concluding the morning announcements at our school, we remind students of three crucial messages we first heard from Jonathan Saphier (2005):

1. The work we do here is important.
2. You can do it.
3. We will not give up on you.

These same three messages apply to school principals and other school leaders. There is, perhaps, no work more important than the work we must do. Although the work is difficult, together we can do it and we must not give up on ourselves or any of our students as we undertake it. Fortunately, Marzano and colleagues (2005) have made the important work we do more *workable*. They have sifted through 69 studies conducted from 1978 to 2001, which examined the relationship between the leadership of the building principal and student academic achievement. These studies involved nearly 3,000 schools of all grade configurations and included approximately 14,000 teachers and 1,400,000 students. Interpreting this exhaustive amount of data, the authors computed the correlation between the leadership behavior of the school principal and the academic achievement of students in the school to be 0.25. Such an effect indicates that an increase in principal leadership behavior from the 50th to the 84th percentile would be accompanied by a gain in the overall achievement of the school from the 50th percentile to the 60th percentile.

Armed with this data, we know what we must do as principals and school leaders. Now, we must go out there and actually do it. Nearly every principal with whom we have ever worked has suggested that a primary reason for entering the arena of educational leadership is the desire to "make a difference." Here, we have clear evidence that what we do can indeed make a very powerful difference and help our students and schools realize higher levels of academic achievement. Knowing that we have such potential to enhance student achievement, it is our responsibility to examine what the research indicates will lead to higher levels of leadership behavior. Our first responsibility, then, is none of the 21 identified through the study cited in this chapter. Instead, our first responsibility is to become aware of what the research indicates and understand how we can use these findings to improve our own performance. We must lead the way in closing the knowing-doing gap as it relates to school leadership.

This book is organized in a way that we hope provides school leaders with a roadmap for improving student and teacher performance within their schools through their own leadership behaviors. First, we begin by asking the reader to determine where they currently are as school leaders by completing a brief leadership self assessment. Next, in each of the following chapters, we hope to provide specific and practical ideas which will assist the reader in developing each of the nine leadership responsibilities. We begin each chapter by first defining the specific leadership responsibility and suggesting how it applies to the daily leadership practices of school principals. Next, in a section we call, Points to Ponder, we offer several strategic ideas that any administrator at the K–12 level can use to fulfill the leadership responsibility under examination. We then summarize these points as our five Core

Components, those leadership actions that are most likely to result in powerful change. Next, we present a fictional narrative providing a glimpse into a day in the life of one school principal, who acts on each responsibility as she performs her regular duties at Cornerstone High School. Following each narrative account, we offer a short Core Reflections page. This space for personal reflection refers readers back to the *core components* of the leadership responsibility, asking them to reflect not only on how the principal in the narrative was able to fulfill the leadership responsibility but also how they, as leaders within their own school, can lead with the purpose of improving teacher and student performance.

The cornerstones for leading our schools more effectively are already in place. These cornerstones of school leadership have been identified through a painstaking process of quantitative data collection and analysis (Marzano, et al., 2005). Now, it is the responsibility of principals desiring to make a difference to put these cornerstones into place at their own schools by transforming these empirical findings into actions, strategic practices which will serve to finally close the knowing-doing gap in the area of school leadership and—more importantly—improve levels of academic achievement for students we serve.

Leadership Self-Assessment

To begin your journey toward fulfilling the leadership responsibilities examined in this book, take a moment to determine your current behaviors, beliefs, actions, and attitudes as they relate to these nine cornerstones of purposeful school leadership. Answer each of the following questions using the scale provided. Don't over think your answers—go with your first instinct. Be as honest as possible. Don't indicate what you think you *should* do; note what you *actually* do. And most importantly, be candid.

4 = Is characteristic of me *nearly all the time.*
3 = Is *usually* characteristic of me.
2 = Is *sometimes* characteristic of me.
1 = Is *rarely* characteristic of me.

_____ 1. I inquire regularly and often.
_____ 2. I remain positive in the midst of anxiety and change.
_____ 3. I am an active participant in my school community.
_____ 4. I reveal my beliefs through my actions.
_____ 5. I have explicit conversations with teachers about their performance.

_____ 6. I am equipped to anticipate needs.

_____ 7. I routinely spend time in classrooms.

_____ 8. I design purposeful and proactive communication with teachers and school community stakeholders.

_____ 9. I promote a sense of well-being among my faculty and staff.

_____ 10. I involve teachers in all aspects of the school's functioning.

_____ 11. I regularly recognize and address school failures.

_____ 12. I consciously set a positive emotional tone.

_____ 13. I foster mutual respect.

_____ 14. I am receptive to negative feedback.

_____ 15. I am committed to and make decisions from a set of ideals and beliefs.

_____ 16. I am easily accessible.

_____ 17. I create structures to promote and sustain professional conversation.

_____ 18. I model the expectations I have of others.

_____ 19. I use my school's mission/values/beliefs to monitor progress.

_____ 20. I have high levels of infectious energy.

_____ 21. I acknowledge significant events in the lives of teachers.

_____ 22. I hold teachers accountable for student achievement.

_____ 23. I consciously choose to spend minimal time in my office.

_____ 24. I am tuned in to my school's undercurrents.

_____ 25. I build the capacity for open dialog among teachers.

_____ 26. I develop common language and common work among my faculty.

_____ 27. I often solicit and readily act on feedback.

_____ 28. I always engage and respond with timely care.

_____ 29. I regularly recognize and celebrate school accomplishments.

_____ 30. I strive for consensus.

_____ 31. I am the driving force behind major initiatives.

_____ 32. I ensure that my school's mission/values/beliefs are a reflection of all school stakeholders.

_____ 33. I communicate and articulate effectively.

_____ 34. I often include teachers in analytical and reflective conversations.

_____ 35. I listen intently.

_____ 36. I regularly attend an array of extracurricular events.

_____ 37. I use teams of teachers for decision making.

_____ 38. I am an active participant in my school's core work.

_____ 39. I regularly recognize, celebrate, and tap talent among my faculty and staff.

_____ 40. I regularly share my beliefs with all school stakeholders.

_____ 41. I inspire others to accomplish things beyond their grasp.

_____ 42. I monitor my actions and words.

_____ 43. I have frequent contact with students and teachers.

_____ 44. I am aware of and act on the personal needs of teachers.

_____ 45. I systematically recognize and celebrate the accomplishments of students.

Now, transfer your answers for each question to the corresponding box on the following score sheet (Figure 1.1). *Add your scores down each column,* and then *add your scores across for a survey total.* A *perfect* score totals 20 in each column for an overall total of 180. Yet, our intent is not to tell you what represents a *good* or *bad* score but to help you discern areas of strengths and areas of needed growth. Therefore, go back and closely examine the category in which you have your lowest score. This is the area that requires your immediate attention. Where is your highest score? This is the area of leadership that represents your greatest strength. In addition, subsequent chapters correlate with each category on the score sheet, so you can reflect on your behavioral strengths and growth areas as you read. And remember, just because you are good at something doesn't mean that you can't pick up a few tips and suggestions provided in *every* chapter.

Figure 1.1 Score Sheet

Chapter 1: Optimizer	Chapter 3: Affirming	Chapter 4: Ideals/Beliefs	Chapter 5: Awareness	Chapter 6: There-ness	Chapter 7: Relationships	Chapter 8: Communicating	Chapter 9: Culture	Chapter10: Input
2	5	4	1	7	3	8	9	10
12	11	15	6	16	13	17	18	14
20	22	19	24	23	21	25	26	27
31	29	32	35	36	34	33	28	30
41	45	40	38	43	44	42	39	37
Total:	Total:	Total:	Total:	Total:	Total:	Total:	Total:	Total:
Overall total for all nine categories (180 possible):								

2

The
Optimizing Leader

Cornerstone #1:

The school principal serves as the school's optimizer by inspiring others and providing an optimistic view of what good the school is already doing, and what it can accomplish in the future to become great.

In endeavoring to identify specific behaviors related to principal leadership that may have a relationship to student academic achievement, Marzano, Waters, and McNulty (2005) identified 21 categories of such behaviors that they refer to as responsibilities of the school leader. The authors posit that 9 of the 21 responsibilities fall under the direct domain of the school principal. An example of such a responsibility directly associated with the principal's role as school leader is what the authors refer to as *optimizer,* which they define as "the extent to which the leader inspires others and is the driving force when implementing a challenging innovation" (p. 56).

Using the preceding definition, it is evident that this responsibility is almost wholly the school principal's. Clearly, the responsibility of inspiring others and serving as the driving force behind change initiatives is of paramount importance. Left unfulfilled, the school principal's prospects for succeeding as an effective leader are bleak. Conversely, serving as an effective optimizer may result in increased student academic achievement. In analyzing 17 research studies involving 724 schools, there was a 0.20 correlation between the responsibility referred to as *optimizer* and student academic achievement (Marzano et al., 2005). Armed with the knowledge that serving as an optimistic leader positively affects student performance, school principals must monitor their behaviors related to this responsibility and find new ways to fulfill this role.

It is, perhaps, just a bit ironic that in a book so thoroughly rooted in quantitative research, the authors of *School Leadership that Works* list the first principal responsibility as optimizer. Although some research clearly suggests a relationship between this responsibility and student achievement, such data are not necessarily required to intuitively understand that the leader of any organization must exude optimism and optimize the efforts of all teachers. Goleman, Boyatzis, and McKee (2002) have written extensively about "emotional intelligence" (EI), exploring the role between EI and leadership. They include optimism as a Leadership Competency within their framework of emotionally intelligent leaders, suggesting that optimistic leaders can roll with the punches and perceive setbacks as opportunities rather than threats. Optimistic leaders see others in a positive light and expect the best from them. Their positive outlook leads them to expect that impending changes are always for the better. Perhaps schools, more than any other organization, need such optimistic leadership, because our customers are young people we are molding to become future leaders themselves.

How then, do principals go about the business of serving as optimizing leaders? It begins with setting expectations and then building relationships so others want to meet those expectations. Leaders are possibility thinkers, not probability thinkers (Kouzes & Posner, 1987). School principals must communicate this important distinction to teachers and students. Based on past performance, we might expect it *probable* that a certain student will fail a course or misbehave. Based on past performance, we might conclude it *probable* that a certain school will not make adequate yearly progress once again or may be perceived as an unsafe school. The principal's job as optimizer is to change some educators' habits of thinking that past performance probably indicates future performance. Instead, we must consider all possibilities and expect the very best outcome. Many fellow coaches and teachers have adopted the adage, "Whether you think you can or think you can't, you are right." Optimizing leaders understand this and realize that if we expect our teachers and students to succeed, chances are greater that they will. Likewise, if we expect our students to fail, they probably will. Optimistic leaders know that our expectations are accurate predictors of student, teacher, and school performance; they affect behaviors throughout the school to the point that they can even overcome seemingly inevitable failure based on low expectations because of past performance. Optimism is contagious; when the school leader is enthusiastic, smiles, listens, jokes, and instills a sense of hope within others, possibilities become more important than probabilities.

The optimizing leader is revealed in a variety of ways. Following are just a few ways we identified that principals can fulfill the responsibility of optimizer as outlined in *School Leadership that Works* (Marzano, et al., 2005). These characteristics, actions, beliefs, and behaviors are described in detail and followed by a brief list of five thoughts summarizing our experiences in this critical area.

The Optimizer: Points to Ponder

Mission, Vision, and Values

In looking to improve school performance, it is common to begin by looking at the school's mission, vision, values, goals, and even its motto. The optimistic leader knows that establishing or revisiting these written documents are a first step toward building hope and a sense of efficacy within the school. A school's mission statement sets the stage for an optimistic learning environment by succinctly and precisely capturing the purpose of the school. Although nearly all schools include the word *learning* within their mission statements, it can be included in many ways, some of which are positive and some which are less so. For example, at one point one of the authors was named assistant principal at an existing elementary school. On his very first visit to this school, he was struck by the prominent and attractive wooden placards that consumed a large wall of the school's foyer. On these placards were listed the school's mission statement and vision. The wording relating to expectations nearly took his breath away—but not because he was overwhelmed by its noble loftiness. In large letters it proclaimed for anyone visiting that "we will be a school with *reasonable* expectations for all." Not surprisingly, this school's results fell into the *reasonable* category also; they had not performed exceptionally, but had produced, well, *reasonably* satisfactory results. Luckily, the new principal assigned to the school also immediately noticed this self-defeating proclamation and had the sign removed as she led the staff in revisiting the school's mission and vision statements.

Instead of settling for mediocrity or vague platitudes in creating statements of vision, mission, values, goals and mottos, leaders must strive for specificity, standards of excellence, and statements that optimistically compel others to expect success and realization of school goals and visions. The best way we know to incorporate strong, specific, and optimistic language into these necessary and important school documents is to include, as DuFour and Eaker (1998) suggest, faculty value statements in addition to mission and vision statements. These are statements the entire school staff develops and commits to as a way to fulfill the school's mission and achieve the school's vision and goals. These statements are extremely powerful because they all begin with two simple, yet forceful words, "We Will." These two words the whole school to action. We suggest limiting these statements to five in number. They should serve as statements by which all faculty members are expected to adhere. Ultimately, these should stand as positive and optimistic standards of behavior for all adults within the school. They move beyond statements focusing on beliefs ("We believe the school should be a safe environment . . ."), into the much more significant realm of *behaviors* and *commitments*. An example of strong and optimistic faculty value statements follow:

- *We Will* promote and insist on a safe and orderly learning environment.
- *We Will* serve as a model for our students by treating all members of our school community with dignity and respect.
- *We Will* produce challenging, engaging lessons that are relevant and meaningful.
- *We Will* not give up on students and will welcome all students regardless of ability or background.
- *We Will* recognize and celebrate our many successes.

The school motto can stand as another simple, yet effective, way to send a positive message to all school stakeholders. Here again, too often such statements are vague and do not necessarily inspire greatness. For example, many schools adopt as their motto a statement such as, "A great place to learn" or "Striving for a great education." Although school mottos tend to be very succinct statements, they should still stand as original and compelling phrases that capture the essence of the school in a fresh way. Two of our favorite school mottos we have seen recently are as follows:

- "Making Learning Irresistible"
- "The Possibilities are Endless"

In just three or four words, each school motto stands as an optimistic phrase that goes beyond triteness and hints ever so slightly at something unique and enduring taking place at the school. Principals can serve as optimizing leaders by ensuring that all public documents, such as school missions, mottos, and visions portray a school that is looking forward to continuous growth and improvement.

Building Teacher Confidence

Another way that school principals can serve as optimistic leaders is simply by placing trust in the school's teachers and giving them confidence in their abilities to succeed in the classroom. Our students succeed when they are confident in their abilities to perform. Our teachers are no different. If they are confident in their lesson plans or abilities to manage the learning environment, their students are much more likely to learn the intended outcomes. Principals can boost the confidence of teachers in many ways.

Perhaps the most effective means for principals to instill teacher confidence is by leading with questions rather than answers. It is probably safe to assume that in every school in our country, teachers occasionally approach the principal to ask what to do about a certain situation, whether it relates to a specific student or parent or a general question about classroom management or teaching and learning. Oftentimes, these are our very finest teachers, who have every bit as much expertise as the principal to whom they are posing the question. When faced with such situations, we have found one particularly effective response to both get to a resolution and instill confidence in the teacher asking advice. The principal simply responds with, "What do you think we should do?" or some similar query, depending on the situation, which invites reflection from the teacher. Inevitably, our best teachers are able to self-reflect and offer ideas every bit as insightful—if not more so—than whatever the principal might suggest. Teachers are more confidence in the plan of action when they are responsible for developing it.

Another way for principals to instill confidence in teachers is by affirming behaviors that clearly uphold the school's mission, vision, and values and lead to student success. Many principals make brief, but regular, visits to classrooms. In doing so, they note what their very best teachers are doing every day. One way to take this a step further is by immediately writing notes to teachers, specifically praising particularly effective techniques observed and placing these notes in their mailboxes before the end of the school day. Faculty meetings are another opportune time to affirm superior performance of our best teachers. Many principals recognize teachers at the end of faculty meetings using a variety of items as *prizes*. Several principals we know order a dozen roses, which are distributed by either administrators or fellow teachers to those colleagues who have demonstrated success in the classroom, taken the lead on a school wide initiative, or maintained perfect attendance for a certain time period. Other principals award certificates, pins, free ice cream passes, or almost any other item to recognize deserving teachers. The reward itself is not nearly as important as the recognition for a job well done that has helped improve the school in some way. Such ceremonial traditions not only instill confidence in these teachers who are working the hardest to improve student achievement, they also help the principal create an optimistic, enthusiastic environment.

Although principals must fulfill the responsibility of school optimizer throughout the school year, it takes on critical importance at the very beginning and then again at the end of the year. At the beginning of the school year, anxiety levels may be high but so are the spirits and outlooks of the teachers. At this point in the year, no student has yet misbehaved and no parent has called to complain. Teachers are eager to begin another year and principals must seize this opportunity to set the stage for a year-long journey of learning. At this time of the year, the principal must clearly highlight exactly what the school is doing well. It is vital that the principal offer quantitative as well as anecdotal evidence documenting these accomplishments. Certainly, the principal should highlight areas found in the standardized testing results that document exceptional learning progress, but it is equally important to offer stories of individual students or parents who had exceptionally positive experiences at the school in the previous years. One veteran principal we know makes it a point during the preplanning week before school begins to read a few letters written by graduating seniors to their teachers. Another collects an assortment of motivational, uplifting, humorous, and challenging quotes and photos from the previous school year and scrolls these on a large screen set to music for teachers to view at the initial faculty meeting of each new school year.

It is imperative at this critical point of the school year to celebrate what has already been accomplished, yet it is equally important to carefully map out what must be accomplished during the current or impending school year to achieve even greater success. Here, principals must confront, as Collins (2001) suggests, the "brutal facts." Even our highest-performing schools can readily identify areas of student achievement that merit close scrutiny and improved results. By clearly identifying these areas, presenting evidence that supports the need for improvement, and openly sharing this information with all teachers, principals begin the process of confronting the current reality and planning for improvement. As the school optimizer, the next step is critical for school leaders: instilling in all teachers the confidence that, together, the school community can set specific goals for improved results in this particular academic area; develop actions, strategies, and interventions to ensure that the goals are realized; and implement a plan and schedule for monitoring the progress of the plan throughout the school year. Saphier (2005) suggests sending three crucial messages to our students:

1. The work we do is important.
2. You can do it.
3. We will not give up on you.

These three crucial messages we send students must also be sent from administrators to teachers. Optimizers let teachers know that the work ahead is not necessarily easy, but it is important work that we can and should undertake with confidence and determination. Just as we would not give up on the students we teach, we must not give up on our teachers or allow teachers to give up on themselves or the implementation of the school's plan for improvement.

Creating a Culture of Care

By now, most everyone has heard the oft-repeated statement that "people want to know how much you care before they care how much you know." Typically in education, we use this phrase to remind ourselves that our students take this approach with their teachers; however, this also holds true in the principal–teacher relationship. Commonly, two principals are equipped with almost identical knowledge regarding an initiative, yet one fails to implement or communicate the change initiative and one succeeds. The variable here is that the successful principal has cultivated positive relationships with teachers, making those teachers more open to the idea of change. Teachers and principals at all levels of education in kindergarten through grade 12 work together for long hours each day throughout the school year. As a result, creating and maintaining caring relationships among the staff becomes of paramount importance. Teachers and administrators who care about each other are much more likely to work together to improve school climate and student achievement.

Principals play the key role in cultivating this climate of caring. Small acts of kindness can often mean a great deal to teachers with whom we work. Throughout the course of a typical school year, a staff inevitably experiences weddings, births, deaths, and holidays, as well as many other unexpected joys and tragedies among its community. The caring principal takes time to recognize all these events and encourages teachers to gather and share in happy and sad moments alike. At our own schools, we have made this a priority. One way we recognize teachers each Christmas season is by sending a holiday greeting card to the parent (or another close relative) of each teacher at our school. Throughout the semester, we take a photo of each teacher, custodian, cafeteria worker, and office staff member working with children and affix this to a greeting card. Inside, we have printed a simple salutation, "We'd like to share one of our valued treasures at our school. She (He) makes our school a better place in which to learn. Happy Holidays!" Each administrator includes a handwritten note on the card to the teacher's parents, and we send these out just before leaving for our holiday break. The first year we did this, almost all teachers made it a point to let us know how much this meant to them and their families, and this has become an antici-pated tradition at our school. An added bonus is that each January we inevi-tably receive many notes in return from our teachers' parents and family members, thanking us for taking the time to recognize their son or daughter in this way.

Although the school year is always filled with many joyous occasions, we have, unfortunately, been faced with many tragedies, as well. At one of our schools, we lost three staff members to cancer in the past 3 years. In addition, a student tragically and unexpectedly passed away. The teachers at this school have created a *butterfly garden* in the courtyard to remember these and other loved ones in our family who we have lost. This garden area includes benches with the names of these teachers and students engraved on nameplates, along with birdhouses, stone monuments, and decorative butterfly figurines. This has become a small, but special, area of our school that many students and teachers visit at some point in the year to sit and enjoy a lunch or just reflect on a friendship and the loss of a loved one. In one instance, a teacher at our school passed away after a valiant battle with cancer. Her will specified that in lieu of flowers or any other remembrances, donations should be made to the school's media center. Ultimately, our staff decided to dedicate the media center in her honor, unofficially naming it after this beloved colleague. Each school's staff is different and handles both celebratory and mournful occasions in their own special way, but the principal must promote a caring climate to ensure that these special moments are shared throughout the school community. Doing so optimizes the natural compassion, caring, and collegiality of teachers and ultimately infuses these same values within our students. When an entire school is filled with people who care about each other, it is likely one also filled with people who care deeply about teaching and learning.

Implementing Change Initiatives

The optimizer must go beyond merely serving with energy, enthusiasm, and an optimistic spirit. The optimizer must—as the term, of course, suggests—make optimal use of every available resource to maximize the effectiveness and efficiency of the organization. Clearly, the most valuable resource is our people, particularly the teachers working within the school. Principals are optimizers when they realize that changes in education are ongoing and necessary yet tend to create stress and even resistance within many teachers. Many schools are changing how they assess student learning as well as the way they handle grading and reporting. Others are moving from traditional schedules to block schedules. With each passing year, new technological innovations are implemented. We are becoming increasingly dependent on data and insisting that all teachers examine data relating to student learning and act based on what they glean from these results. In the midst of these and numerous other changes facing educators, the principals' responses are critical and perhaps the most important way they serve as optimizers. The principal must first sift through all possible changes that can be made at any school at any given point in time to determine which is merely another *flavor of the month* idea versus those that might truly influence student learning. If the change under consideration does not directly and positively affect student achievement, the likelihood of the change initiative succeeding is slim at best. The optimizing principal must scrutinize all available research related to changes actually adopted and implemented to inform teachers that the need for change exists, the change initiative addresses this need, and the entire school must be committed to change.

The authors have led schools through a variety of change initiatives ranging from structural changes relating to scheduling, discipline, and school safety to larger, more cultural changes such as moving schools forward as true professional learning communities. Successfully implementing change initiatives requires that we follow a plan designed to produce steady progress toward our goal; we do this by focusing on five actions: (1) informing, (2) energizing, (3) committing, (4) supporting, and (5) monitoring. In considering the first three actions, we tend to focus on our very finest teachers first, typically working through our school's leadership team, comprised of many of our schools' most respected teacher leaders. If our best teacher leaders agree that the change is needed and will prove beneficial to student learning, chances are good that others within the school will willingly follow suit. If our most effective teachers are not convinced, chances are slim that the rest of the staff will commit to change. More importantly, if our most respected teachers are not convinced that the proposed change is wise, we, as principals, should reexamine our own conclusions before trying to move forward at all.

We must first *inform* these key stakeholders why a need for change exists and what possible solutions are available, providing as much empirical and anecdotal evidence as possible. Once we provide information pertaining to the current status at our schools along with various strategies, actions, and programs we might implement, we must *energize* our teacher leaders to examine, analyze, and synthesize data and information. Most importantly, perhaps, we must invite them to share their own ideas and perhaps offer additional strategies for improving the specific need area under consideration. Once all options have been thoroughly discussed, principals, together with the entire leadership team, must *commit* to a specific plan for improvement and for presenting the plan to the entire staff for school wide implementation. At this stage of the process, it is important to remember that, to move forward in presenting the plan to the entire faculty, we need a strong consensus, rather than unanimity. Despite our earlier warnings suggesting we heed the advice of our superior teacher leaders, we must also realize that unanimous consent—particularly in considering significant changes—is the exception, rather than the rule. Our very best teachers realize this, too, and accept the consensus decision of a strong team of respected peers. Each leadership team member must agree to passionately and positively represent all aspects of the improvement initiative to their own team members in preparation for school wide adoption.

The next stage of the process requires the most effort and steadfast commitment. As principals, we must take the lead in letting all teachers know why we are moving in a certain direction. Principals must acknowledge the challenges and obstacles that are almost certainly ahead and listen carefully to the concerns teachers may have about the time and effort required on their part in implementing a new initiative. Yet, they must be relentless in responding to let everyone know that they, along with the school's leadership team, have studied the problem at length and carefully determined a course of action. Although principals must listen carefully and respond to all concerns, again they must realize that not all staff members follow immediately and enthusiastically; however, most understand, accept, and work to implement the plan. From this point forward, through the end of the school year and beyond, the principal best supports all teachers by *supporting* and *monitoring* their efforts.

Support comes in many ways. Certainly, the principal must plan to expend financial support in terms of materials, resources, and professional development funding. More importantly, though, the principal must support teachers in a way that is less expensive financially but much more *expensive* in terms of effort: The principal must *be there* for teachers throughout the process, sitting in on meetings, visiting classrooms, individually talking with teachers, and listening to teachers discuss what they are learning. In a word, principals must *monitor* the progress of the plan. Too often, the word *monitor* in such situations carries a negative connotation. We maintain that, when done well, it is perceived as a positive, both by teachers and principals. Teachers should come to see that having principals monitor their progress is indeed a form of support, and principals must learn that this type of support is much more valuable, and more demanding, than any amount of financial support. Throughout this stage and in the ensuing months, it is more important that the principal focus the most efforts on the most willing teachers, rather than the reluctant ones. No amount of support will gain the commitment of every teacher in the building, but it is imperative that we support teachers who are leading the way or at least approaching the plan with an open mind. By *informing, energizing, committing, supporting,* and *monitoring,* principals act to optimize the efforts of all teachers within the school and ensure that new initiatives are planned and implemented as effectively as possible.

Core Components

The preceding bulleted points include just a few varied ways that school principals serve as their schools' optimizing leader. Whether talking about significant optimizing actions such as leading an entire school through a wide scale cultural shift or less sophisticated, but equally important optimizing actions, such as letting teachers know that you care about them, principals must realize that these actions have many positive consequences. One such consequence is not realized immediately and can be rather subtle, but stands as the most important of all: *Student learning increases.*

In reviewing the short list of ideas offered above, we determined that they fall into one or more of the following five categories, which seem to succinctly encapsulate what we see as the core components of the *optimizing leader*:

Cornerstone #1: Optimizer
1. *Promote the Positives:*   Optimizing principals should find and communicate positives first, because even the growth derived from a less-than-positive experience can be productively viewed and used.
2. *Open Invitation:*   Optimizing principals realize that it only takes the extension of one to move another to new or higher ground, because a single invitation validates and signifies confidence and desired belonging.
3. *Be What You Aspire To Be:*   Optimizing principals reveal their quintessential selves to others every day, sharing their core values, goals, and visions. Intentional and unintentional followers are inspired to aspire themselves.
4. *Recognize and Celebrate:*   Optimizing principals regularly honor major and minor success, both in individual and collective efforts, and also share in the sorrows and disappointments that inevitably arise.
5. *Get Rooted:*   Optimizing principals serve as more than cheerleaders when planning and implementing change. They are rooted in the change itself, reading and learning so that they can propel the core work.

Typically, there is no such thing as a *typical* day in the life of the school principal. The responsibilities that must be carried out each day are vast, challenging, multifarious, and cannot always be planned on a daily schedule. Yet, despite the many events, both planned and unanticipated, that occur throughout the principal's day, one constant remains: the core focus must always be student achievement. The optimizing leader plans for and responds to events during the day, which reveals this focus and exhibits a relentless quest to instill this focus in others within the school. The following anecdotal illustration provides a brief snapshot how principals optimize the efforts of all as they moves throughout the day.

A Glimpse of the Optimizing Principal

"What have you learned today?" asks Natalie Parker, third-year principal at Cornerstone High School, as she composes her Monday morning e-mail to a faculty of 150 entering the last full school week before final exams and winter break. In today's e-mail, Natalie challenges the faculty to pose this question to their students as well as themselves at the close of each day. In addition, she includes reminders of today's Leadership Team meeting, college visit during lunch, second-semester class recommendations, and the necessary preparations for the following day's PLC (Professional Learning Community) sessions. Natalie also compliments the academic bowl team on last night's win and adds a special note of congratulations to teachers Henry Gill and Lucy Peterson who recently completed their Master's degrees. She concludes with an invitation to *Teach and learn with passion!*

Without hesitation, Natalie opens her Outlook calendar to review the day ahead. Her schedule includes a fourth-block visit to Anna Klein's *spirited* ninth-grade physical science class, and a parent conference with Mr. Delatorre, her neighbor, at 10:15 a.m. Printing the day's calendar, Natalie stands to greet head custodian Harvey Nichols to discuss last night's unplanned alarm as well as the details of Thursday's custodian appreciation lunch that the school's Sunshine Committee is preparing.

After thanking Harvey for his quality work, Natalie returns to her office to check voice mails and handwrite two brief notes of appreciation: One is to a mentor teacher stating, "Thank you for taking the time to model classroom instruction that everyone wants to emulate. Your ability to build a caring rapport with your colleagues has not gone unnoticed and is genuinely appreciated." The other is to another teacher

---

Natalie has overheard complaining about PLC work: "Thank you for the insightful feedback you provided your colleagues on your peer observations; as a result, I noticed that Lynn Grimes is using your assessment suggestion. More teachers could benefit from your assessment expertise, and I'd like you to consider joining the Standards Team this semester as they work on creating performance rubrics. You would have much to offer. Thanks for considering and letting me know."

After placing each card in its respective mailbox, Natalie picks up her highlighted copy of Steve Farber's *The Radical Leap: A Personal Lesson in Extreme Leadership* (2004) and a small bag filled with Partners in Education coupons as she heads out to meet her weekly, voluntary book study group joining 12 teachers and paraprofessionals already chatting about today's reading. Natalie is excited to hear what the others have to say about her favorite part of the book: generating energy.

In the middle of the morning rush, Natalie stops to ask Kathy Dalton, counseling secretary, how she and her family are coping with the loss of Kathy's father. She hugs Kathy and encourages more time off campus with family, if needed. With a smile, Natalie enters through Cornerstone's front doors under a large, scrolling digital sign that proudly announces, "Through these doors walk the finest people in the world: our students, their parents, our faculty, and our guests."

Warmly welcomed by the front office secretary Carla Natalie jokes with their senior office aide and encourages her to take part in the Student Advisory Council (SAC) to work on school-related issues and improvements. The SAC is currently creating an *Expectations From Cornerstone's Graduates* guide to be shared with rising ninth-grade students and their parents during spring middle school transition meetings. Natalie looks forward to getting feedback from Cornerstone's feeder middle school principals at their upcoming monthly cluster meeting.

After the 2-minute, first-block announcements, Natalie walks nearly every hallway of Cornerstone High, sharing smiles, visiting classes, and inquiring about students and teachers along the way. In classes, she looks for learning readiness, standards in action, meaningful work, engaged students, active teaching, collaboration, class climate, questions posed, patterns of behavior, lessons, pedagogy, and early warnings of problems to come. Outside classes, she monitors bathroom passes, notices the condition of facilities, redirects lingering students, and stops in the faculty workroom to share in the frustration of a misbehaving copier.

Wiping black toner from her hands, Natalie eases into Stephanie Walker's classroom to review and finalize plans for tomorrow's PLC meetings during planning blocks. To assist, Natalie suggests a quick review of both the school's instructional *non-negotiables* derived by whole-faculty consensus early in the school year and Chapter 6 in Anne Davies' *Making Classroom Assessment Work* (2000). Yet, after hearing Stephanie's concern regarding "teacher overload," Natalie agrees that the chapter review should be cut from the plans. As she leaves Natalie hands Stephanie the small bag of Partners in Education dinner coupons to be given out to all teachers being honored with a peer-nominated *Commendable Cougar* award during each PLC. Under Stephanie's leadership, this year's Standards Team of teachers has taken genuine ownership in planning, organizing, and delivering PLC lessons.

Thereafter, Natalie heads outside to the commons area to monitor transition between classes; and she meets an early-arriving Mr. Delatorre, inviting him into her office. Seated next to him, Natalie asks, "How can I assist you today?" and listens carefully to his list of concerns regarding his son's geometry teacher, Mr. Bell. Natalie offers Mr. Delatorre her intimate knowledge of Mr. Bell's instructional and grading practices, Monday and Wednesday help sessions, and collaborative work with his geometry team. Assured by Natalie's awareness and care, Mr. Delatorre decides to take Natalie's advice and contact Mr. Bell regarding the class and his son's performance therein and leaves fully informed of Cornerstone's cohesive practices, beginning with the principal.

Walking Mr. Delatorre out, Natalie turns her door sign to "Out Learning," and reminds Carla that she will be in classrooms for the remainder of second block. Carla knows that except for an emergency, Natalie wants her scheduled time in classrooms to be uninterrupted, as do the teachers and students she visits.

Energized about the lessons and quality learning found in classrooms throughout the school, in addition to reflecting on how to approach Ms. Carpenter after witnessing a "free day" in her class, Natalie monitors the hallway between the media center and the gym during transition to third block.

Back in her office, Natalie calls the principal of Creekview High in an effort to calibrate next steps of their county's High School Improvement Plan. Committed to the county's plan, they exchange ideas, possibilities, data, and projected responses regarding the transition back to the traditional seven-period day before taking their thoughts on how to best accomplish such back to their respective Leadership Teams for input. As a result, Natalie is hopeful that all county high school teachers will embrace the schedule change.

Excited about the scheduling possibilities and student learning potential that coincides with the seven-period day, Natalie welcomes Sarah Carpenter into her office. Sarah apologizes for the free day Natalie observed while visiting her second block today and explains that she was ahead of her world geography colleagues and wanted to give the other world geography classes a chance to "catch up." Yet, after a conversation reminding Sarah of a particular Cornerstone value statement ensuring engaging and meaningful lessons every day for every student, Sarah apologizes and asks Natalie to visit her classes tomorrow. Natalie thanks Sarah for her conscientiousness and looks forward to seeing the good work and learning that usually transpires under Sarah's guidance.

Purposely monitoring the halls near Ms. Anna Klein's science class, Natalie informally talks with students and teachers regarding final exams and holiday plans ahead before the fourth-block tardy bell rings. Natalie takes a seat in the back of Ms. Klein's physical science class and notices a few students from Sarah Carpenter's second-block class, including Robert Delatorre, unprepared when class begins. After taking many discreet notes consisting of classroom management positives and suggestions for improvement, Natalie leaves a thank you note on Anna's desk. Within, Natalie encourages Anna to "keep up the immediate positive feedback" and that she will follow up with Anna in detail during her first-block planning tomorrow.

At the end of the day Natalie invites every Cornerstone teacher and student to "extend your learning, yourself, and your heart" beyond the class day and anticipates everyone's "safe return to school tomorrow" over the afternoon announcements.

Core Reflections

Consider the ideal *optimizing* actions of Principal Parker and use the space provided to jot down examples of each core component found within this glimpse. Next, reflect on your own optimizing leadership actions and include personal notes affirming your strengths and areas of needed growth.

Cornerstone #1: Optimizer
1. Promote the Positives:
2. Open Invitation:
3. Be What You Aspire To Be:
4. Recognize and Celebrate:
5. Get Rooted:
Personal Notes:

3

Affirming Success (and Acknowledging Failure)

Cornerstone #2:

The school principal fulfills the responsibility of affirmation by recognizing and celebrating school accomplishments and acknowledging and addressing school failures. The principal systematically and fairly addresses both successes and failures within the school.

The second leadership responsibility identified by Marzano, Waters, and McNulty (2005), which fall directly under the purview of the school principal and ultimately relate to student achievement, is called *affirmation*. The authors define *affirmation* as "the extent to which the leader recognizes and celebrates school accomplishments—and acknowledges failures" (p. 41). In analyzing six quantitative research studies examining 332 schools related to this school leadership theme, the authors found an overall correlation of 0.19 between the leadership responsibility of affirmation and student academic achievement. Although many within the school can join in recognizing and celebrating successes, it is up to the school principal to establish this as a priority and encourage its practice. In the case of acknowledging failure, this portion of the affirmation responsibility is even more clearly the domain of the principal. Both, however, are vital to the success of any school in terms of student learning.

At first glance, affirmation appears at least indirectly related to the first cornerstone of school success, *optimizer*. A component of each is recognizing and celebrating the good that has occurred and continues to exist within the school. Like each of the nine cornerstones we examine in this book, that of affirmation carries with it aspects that are more technical in nature and require understanding of educational leadership as well as a human relations component, which can only be addressed successfully by school leaders who truly care about others and enjoy working with people of diverse backgrounds, skills, and personalities. Like optimizer, the responsibility of affirmation also contains within in it a deeper responsibility than the school leader may first discern. Simply serving as an optimistic and enthusiastic principal does not fulfill the role of the optimizer. Instead, the principal must also confront and address the need for change and optimize the efforts of all within the school to ensure embedded change occurs and the school collectively moves forward. A similar situation exists relating to the responsibility of affirmation. The first, more superficial, aspect of affirmation is relatively painless; and many principals embrace and look forward to it: recognizing and celebrating the school's accomplishments. It is the second characteristic of affirmation that requires more courage as well as more effort: addressing the school's failures.

Michael Fullan (2003) considers this latter aspect of affirmation a moral imperative for school leaders. In our own experience, we have yet to come across successful principals who actually enjoy conflict within their schools and gleefully and eagerly confront underperforming teachers. Yet, a difference exists in this area between successful principals at all levels and less successful principals: Although they may not relish the idea, successful principals carry out this important responsibility consistently; less successful principals do not. Often, these less successful principals fail to uphold this responsibility out of kindness and with good intentions, not because they are incompetent or unaware. Yet, as Fullan (2003) suggests, "Conflict avoidance in the face of poor performance is an act of moral neglect" (p. 32).

Moral leaders face the responsibility of acknowledging failure head on, yet know that a key to succeeding in this delicate balancing act of school leadership is ensuring that successes are recognized and celebrated as well. Effective school principals leading strong schools consistently and fairly follow through on both affirmation responsibilities. Principals loyal *only* to their staff may recognize and celebrate school successes regularly yet avoid more difficult conversations with ineffective or underperforming teachers. Principals loyal to *students* recognize and celebrate teacher and school successes but also acknowledge and address failure when it occurs.

Affirming leaders reveal themselves to be so in a variety of ways. Following are just a few ways we have found for principals to fulfill the responsibility of affirmation as outlined in *School Leadership that Works*. We begin by sharing our favorite ways for affirming school successes and follow with ideas on how best to acknowledge and address subpar school and individual performance. These characteristics, actions, beliefs, and behaviors are described in some detail and then followed by a brief list of five thoughts summing up our experiences in this critical area.

Affirmation: Points to Ponder

Teacher Recognition

As we recognize and celebrate successes within our schools, we most certainly honor both individual and school-wide accomplishments. Even in recognizing individual teachers, however, we have found that such recognition must in some way relate to the values, goals, traits, and visions that are commonly shared among the entire staff. Many schools in recent years have adopted lofty and laudable mission, vision, values, and beliefs statements. Too often, however, once adopted, these statements are simply displayed throughout the school (for awhile anyway) and forgotten. One way we *keep the mission alive* at our school is to recognize one teacher each quarter who has worked beyond expectations to fulfill our own school's mission, which suggests, in part, that our teachers do whatever it takes to teach, inspire, and motivate all learners. While principal at this middle school, Jeff Zoul started wearing red high-top Converse sneakers to school with his typical business suit. This became a small phenomenon at the school, particularly among students who seemed to enjoy this odd combination. Partly as a result of this, we decided to name our quarterly mission award the *Red Shoe Award for Walking the Extra Mile*. During a faculty meeting, recipients are presented with a wall plaque, complete with a miniature red high-top sneaker attached and an engraved plate that reads, "Thank you for walking the extra mile to make a difference at our school." Prior to presenting the plaque, we show a video clip or PowerPoint slideshow highlighting the honoree in action with quotes from students and colleagues praising his or her work. In a short amount of time, this has become a highly valued tradition at our school.

Although the mission award goes to an individual, inevitably this individual is one among many who has upheld the mission of the school. Although selected by the administrative team each quarter, the recipient has always earned wide respect among the entire staff for always doing what is right for our students. Teachers who have received this recognition have hosted extra study sessions before and after school or even on Saturdays. They have voluntarily worked with our students most at risk during the summer so that these students retain what they have learned throughout the school year and stay involved in their own learning. They have spent countless hours working with colleagues, sharing new strategies, working out technology kinks, observing in other classrooms, and modeling best practices in their own classrooms. They have sponsored extracurricular activities and coached athletic teams after and before school. In short, they have lived our mission to its fullest and we choose to publicly affirm their behaviors which uphold our shared purpose.

Recently, we began another tradition at our school to honor individual teachers, which we call the *Teacher Hall of Fame*. Although the mission award can be, and has been, awarded to first year as well as veteran teachers, induction into the Teacher Hall of Fame is reserved for teachers who have made a significant and positive difference at our school over an extended period of time. Minimum requirements include 5 consecutive years of teaching at our school with a proven track record of affecting student achievement and exhibiting leadership skills both within and outside their own classroom. Much like the Major League Baseball Hall of Fame, as a school we solicit nominations each year for induction into the *Hall*. Typically, this list starts with 10 or so deserving candidates who qualify for induction. The school leadership team pares this down to five finalists and the entire school then votes on no more than two teachers who are then added to our Hall of Fame at the close of each school year.

In a short amount of time, this way of recognizing and affirming teaching excellence has affected our school. Even teachers who for various reasons have consistently declined the opportunity to be named our school's Teacher of the Year have embraced the idea of being inducted into the Hall of Fame. To permanently honor these recipients, we have displayed in gold letters, "Our Teacher Hall of Fame" along a prominent wall of our school. Underneath these letters, we display a framed photograph of the teacher working with students, along with a plaque briefly recognizing a few highlights from an illustrious career. Much like our mission award, this recognition is individual, yet manages to honor all teachers at our school in that these are educators who are widely respected within our entire school community and are representative of the values created, shared, and adhered to by the entire staff.

Several years ago, many schools and organizations in our area engaged employees in reading books and watching videos based on the *FISH!* Philosophy (Lundin, Paul, & Christensen, 2000) as a way to improve the organization's morale and, ultimately, its performance. The four tenets of this *philosophy* include (1) play, (2) make their day, (3) be there, and (4) choose your attitude. At our schools, we spend a great deal of time immersing our teachers in digging through data as well as current educational research, an extremely important and necessary—if not glamorous—part of school improvement. Conversely, the FISH! movement, is simply an enjoyable way to remind ourselves that our work can be and should be fun and that the relationships we build—with our students, our parents, and each other—are the true key to our success in all other areas. Rather than just read the books, watch the videos, and move on, we try to remind ourselves throughout the school year to keep these four simple phrases in mind and practice them in our daily lives. There are several ways that we do this as a staff.

Faculty meetings are important at our school and are used, in large part, to affirm the good work that we are doing collectively and individually. At the close of each faculty meeting, we present our *Fish Awards*. The awards themselves are worth almost nothing: At each meeting we bring a dozen wrapped gifts containing a package of Swedish Fish candy and Goldfish crackers to give out. Although the gifts themselves are insignificant, they mean a great deal because, unlike some of our other recognitions, these are awarded spontaneously by teachers who choose to stand up and recognize a staff member who has *been there* for a student or a colleague. Teachers have recognized each other in this fashion hundreds of times over the years for a wide variety of reasons; and we always run out of Fish Awards quickly, because teachers rush to the front of the room to honor their colleagues in this fun way. Publicly acknowledging one another for our extra efforts has become an energizing way to close faculty meetings.

During our faculty meetings we also honor—in a literal sense—the FISH! philosophy of *being present*. One of our assistant principals is proficient at establishing business partnerships with local merchants. One way these business partners help our school is by donating gift certificates, which we award at each meeting to teachers who have maintained perfect attendance. Our assistant principal places the names of all teachers with perfect attendance into a hat and we draw six or seven names of lucky winners who receive gift certificates to restaurants and stores as well as for the always-popular free massage! Although this is a fun and random way to offer a few nice gifts to teachers, it actually affirms one of our most important beliefs: Teachers at our school make a huge difference in the lives of our students. Our students learn more when teachers are present each day. Both learning and behavior suffer when our regular teachers are absent. Not surprisingly, our very best teachers have exemplary attendance each and every year. They expect their students to attend school every day and model this behavior themselves. Awarding regular gift certificates for perfect teacher attendance is a small way of acknowledging our teachers who know that their presence makes a difference. Doing this during faculty meetings reinforces the fact that this is a core value and helps to achieve an overarching goal suggested by Whitaker (2003) for all faculty meetings: to make teachers more excited about teaching when they leave the meeting than they were when they arrived.

Another way we keep the spirit of this philosophy alive is through something we call *Pete the Perch*. This is a traveling award that is passed along every 2 or 3 weeks from one teacher to another as a way to recognize a colleague who has worked hard to make our school a better place to teach and learn. Whoever is awarded Pete at the end of the year takes care of him over the summer and awards him to someone else at our very first meeting of the new school year. From that point on, teachers who pass Pete along send an e-mail out to the entire staff, letting everyone know who they are sending him to as well as the reasons why. Once again, the prize itself is inconsequential: we use an old rubber fish that we have been passing along for years now, but teachers typically include a few other small gifts to accompany Pete. However, the e-mails teachers send chronicling the reasons for this recognition make everyone aware of outstanding deeds performed and remind us just how valuable each individual is to the entire school community. Over the years many of our teachers, custodians, cafeteria workers, and office staff have enjoyed hosting Pete for a few weeks before sending him off swimming to a new locale.

Celebrating Student Success

In addition to recognizing and celebrating the accomplishments of teachers, affirming principals must also recognize and celebrate the successes of students (Marzano, et al., 2005). Like almost all schools, we plan for a variety of periodic recognition programs for students at our schools. Although nearly all of these ceremonies recognize students for work directly related to academic achievement, one of our most successful recognition programs highlights positive student behavior. We call this our *Positive Discipline Referral* program. This is an easy and effective way for teachers to recognize students for any reason whatsoever. The referral may be made for specific classroom behaviors, outstanding work, solid citizenship, involvement in extracurricular activities, caring about a teacher or classmate, or showing school spirit. Although teachers are not required to complete and turn in any positive discipline referrals, each year at our school, the most teachers turn in several. In a school of more than 900 students, we typically receive 350 positive discipline referrals each year. Not surprisingly, included in this total are some of our best all-around students, who are recognized for consistently strong performance in all areas. However, the program is equally effective in recognizing our students with the most challenging behavior issues: In many cases, the simple act of completing a positive discipline referral has produced significant improvements in the behavior of our most chronic misbehaving students.

The procedure of completing a positive discipline referral is simple. We created a rather rudimentary two-part carbonless form, which looks very similar to a *regular* discipline referral form, a sample of which follows:

Otwell Middle School
Positive Discipline Referral

Student Name: _____

Referring Teacher: _____

Date of Referral: _____

Reason for Referral: _____

_____

_____

_____

_____

_____

_____

_____

_____

_____

_____

_____

_____

_____

_____

_____

_____

Action Taken by Principal: _____

_____

_____

_____

_____

_____

Teacher Signature	Student Signature	Principal Signature

Teachers simply complete the form and turn it in to the principal, rather than any of the assistant principals. Almost always, students assume the worst as they walk into the office, thinking they are in some sort of major trouble. When students finally realize they have been recognized for a positive behavior of some sort, they immediately brighten. After explaining the referral to the student, we always call a parent to share the good news; award the student a free ice cream, school pen, or school magnet; and mail a copy of the referral to the home. This program has grown to become one of the most popular things we do as a school. Although we enjoy the accolades we have received from the community since we began this practice, we are even more pleased that we are affirming the behaviors we are seeking for all our students.

In addition to recognizing student behavior, we also find ways to systematically recognize and celebrate student attendance and academic achievement. Earlier, we offered our core belief that exemplary teacher attendance is related to student achievement. Of course, student attendance is every bit as important as teacher attendance; and we recognize perfect student attendance in small, but regularly scheduled, ways. Each month, our attendance secretary randomly selects 10 students at each grade level who have achieved perfect attendance for the month. We call these students to the office to receive a small recognition of some sort, usually donated by our business partners. At the end of each semester, we recognize all students who have maintained perfect attendance for the entire semester with a special ceremony and certificate. In both instances the reward itself is insignificant, but we have found that regularly stressing and talking about what we value translates into results. After making a concerted and collective effort to simply remind students throughout the year of our expectations in the area of student attendance, we improved from being the school with the lowest student attendance rate in our district to that with the highest rate of student attendance.

Like most schools we have also created and scheduled various methods of recognizing students for academic success. Although individual teachers, teams of teachers, and departments regularly celebrate such accomplishments in numerous and various ways, as a school we focus on three primary recognition rituals. Our *Breakfast of Champions* ceremony is held after each semester and recognizes students who have earned Honor Roll or Merit Roll status. We mail letters home inviting students and their parents to a short ceremony and breakfast just before school to celebrate academic achievement, our school's core business. We also hold quarterly *PRIDE* ceremonies in our cafeteria, honoring 25 students from each grade level who have excelled in the area of academics and citizenship. Again, we host this event in the morning, inviting parents to join us as we recognize our students with a PRIDE pin, certificate, and trophy. We always invite a speaker from the community to congratulate the students and share a few thoughts on what it takes to succeed in life. We take photos of each student, which we display in a trophy case for the entire quarter until the next recipients are named.

A final way that we, as a school, recognize student academic achievement is through our *Shining Star* program. Although the Breakfast of Champions and PRIDE ceremonies typically recognize our most consistently stellar students in terms of academic achievement, with our Shining Star program we make an effort to target those students who may struggle at times but who have made great strides in terms of grades, behavior, or test scores. We hold this ceremony each month in our media center during lunch and provide students with pizza, cookies, and drinks. We recognize the accomplishments of these students with a certificate and pin and always have one of our valued business partner representatives on hand to share a few words of wisdom with our rising stars.

Each of the preceding student recognition programs is designed to affirm the performances we are expecting for all students in terms of behavior, attendance, and academic achievement. Although they all require effort and planning on the part of the school, they are relatively simple ways of regularly and systematically recognizing students. Each of the preceding ideas can easily be implemented at the elementary, middle, or high school level, although principals would adjust each slightly based on the grade levels being served.

Affirming Schoolwide Success

In addition to recognizing and celebrating individual teacher and student accomplishments, we also must affirm the positive collective performances of the entire school. One way we do this is through the many permanent and temporary displays that decorate all areas of our campus. In our schools the halls and common areas are lined with hundreds of photos showing our students and teachers learning together. We also have a gallery of student photography created as part of our school's photography club. In both our office area and our cafeteria, we have our school motto, *The Possibilities are Endless* prominently displayed. In the cafeteria this motto is surrounded by hundreds of college and university pennants as a way to get our students thinking about future possibilities in terms of their own education.

Although these permanent displays help to communicate our beliefs and share our successes, our temporary displays of student work are even more telling in this area. Schlechty (2002) suggests that schools deeply committed to engaging students in quality work should focus on 12 standards. Standard eight refers to what he calls "Affirmation of Performance" and calls for all persons significant in the lives of students to observe, participate, and benefit from student performances and the products of those performances. This requires a multifaceted approach to *displaying* student work. Of course, nearly every classroom and hallway in our school is covered with displays of student work. Teachers are encouraged to display that work that most clearly illustrates the intended learning outcomes and our students' mastering of them. In addition to this obvious form of celebrating student success through displaying student work, we also encourage a partnership between the elementary, middle, and high schools in our system so that students from each level can work with and learn from students both ahead of them and behind them in the spectrum of kindergarten through grade 12. Students from the high school mentor students at the elementary and middle schools. Students at the middle school write and illustrate children's stories, which they share as they visit elementary classrooms. Students at the elementary school visit both the middle and high schools to *take flight* in a model space shuttle, observe our drama and choir students performing, or conduct a tour of our history museum temporarily set up in our media center. Involving students of all ages in each other's learning is one of the most effective ways we celebrate their learning.

Involving parents in their child's learning is another critical way we affirm the performance of our students. One of the most successful ways we have accomplished this is through our student-led conferences. In these conferences students, rather than teachers, take the lead in showing and telling their parents what they have learned by a given point in the school year. Students guide parents through portfolios and electronic presentations of the work they have produced which represents their mastery of learning outcomes. The number one benefit we have discovered from student-led conferences is the extent to which students become accountable for their own education. Many of us who have taught for years recognize the statement that the best way to truly learn something is by teaching it. Students learn even more as they *teach* their parents what they have already successfully learned and share their goals for future learning. Student-led conferences also increase parent attendance at conference time. We have found that parents are much more likely to attend conferences at which their students are active participants. Having parents recognize and celebrate their child's learning in this way helps to affirm the significance of the student's work for both the student and the parent.

The primary way we recognize and celebrate our school's performance as an entire staff results from what we call our *data digs*. At the close of each year and throughout the summer, this involves scrutinizing every available piece of data we can gather, including data related to school processes, demographics, perceptions, and of course student learning. Using these multiple measures of data (Bernhardt, 1998), we examine enrollment patterns, attendance rates; socioeconomic factors; effectiveness of school programs; perceptions of student, teachers, parents, and community members; and performance on a wide variety of standardized tests, disaggregating this performance to analyze results among our many subgroups. Typically, these data digs reveal many successes as well as a few failures. Although we address how we acknowledge and respond to our failures later, we first focus on our successes.

According to Robbins and Alvy (2003), "In a community of learners, learning is valued and celebrated publicly" (p. 32). At our schools we do this in many of the ways previously outlined. An additional way we do this as an entire staff is through our end of the year *Data Dig Discoveries and Declarations.* During these whole-faculty celebrations and reporting sessions, teams of teachers working throughout the year highlight their successes in the area of student learning as evidenced by the data. The administrative team may highlight survey results of the staff which show that their school scored well above all other elementary schools in the district in terms of school culture, leadership, professional learning, and planning and organization. A team of eighth-grade language arts teachers might share results of the eighth-grade writing assessment, which show the highest percentage of students exceeding standards in the past 10 years. A team of high school science teachers may share results showing that the school's graduation test performance in the area of science was among the top 10 high schools in the state. A team of counselors may show how student attendance rose dramatically from the previous year. Each team of educators is required to not only celebrate their accomplishments but also to provide data which documents this success. Typically, each team of teachers takes between 15 and 25 minutes to present their findings in front of the entire faculty. By having different grade levels, subject areas, and teams share their results with the entire faculty, we are able to foster a sense of ownership for learning in all areas by all staff members.

At our middle school, one small way we recognize and celebrate the importance of all we have learned leading up to our year-end standardized tests as well as the tests themselves is through our faculty *Dress Your Best* days. During these five days of standardized testing, each teacher in the entire school is involved in some way with administering or proctoring the tests. During the time that students are testing, all teachers are "dressed their best." Although teachers at our school typically dress in a casually professional attire, on test days, all male staff members tend to wear a jacket, neckties, and dress slacks and all female teachers wear professional dresses, skirts, and business suits. This is a subtle acknowledgement to our students that their performance on our standardized tests is something we take very seriously, and we honor their best efforts by dressing our very best. Our students enjoy seeing even our most casual teachers dressed to the nines for testing days as an affirmation of its importance in the lives of our students and our entire school.

Acknowledging Failure

Recognizing and celebrating the many successes which occur in our schools is rather easy and painless, especially when compared with the other component of affirmation: acknowledging and responding to our failures. Although not nearly as enjoyable, an equally important responsibility of the school principal is addressing negative performance issues. This is never a comfortable thing to do, but effective principals systematically and fairly address such issues on an individual basis with teachers and students as well as with the school as a whole.

Teacher Underperformance

In acknowledging school wide areas of concern, we begin, of course, by revisiting our data digs, specifically trying to find areas in which we did not meet our goals, performed below expectations, or scored lower than schools with comparable demographic characteristics. As we begin to share these findings with staff, we suggest the following approach which we call, "Go small, go big, go small again, then go individual." That is, we begin by presenting the areas of negative performance with a small group of staff members, our school's leadership team. With this group of school leaders, we confront in a very honest and open manner the brutal facts before us (Collins, 2001) attempting to expose those areas that are undeniably below where they should be, whether it is in the area of student learning, student or teacher attendance, number of discipline referrals, graduation rate, or performance of a student subgroup. We endeavor to present these facts in as honest a manner as possible and lay out two ground rules for doing so:

1. No one is allowed to ignore, explain away, or deny the unpleasant facts before us.

2. We look to accept responsibility rather than assign blame.

Once we accomplish this as our purpose, we begin the process of creating a plan for improvement.

After lengthy analysis, discussion, and brainstorming with the school leadership team, we then *go big*, that is, we present our findings to the entire faculty, making every staff member aware of our few (no more than five) areas of identified underperformance and inviting all staff to share strategies for addressing these need areas and to formulate goals (again, no more than five) for the impending school year. This, of course, takes a fair amount of time and must begin as soon as possible, even before the close of the current school year and throughout the summer. After formulating a plan for improvement, we must then *go small* again, which in our schools means carrying out the work of our school improvement plan within our school's professional learning communities. After assigning each teacher in the school to one or more professional learning communities, the principal must then provide time each week to ensure that these teams of teachers meet and monitor each team's work by sitting in on meetings periodically as well as reading and responding to weekly feedback logs.

Working with and monitoring these small groups continues throughout the school year. As performance issues inevitably arise during this time, the principal must then *go individual,* that is, address the unacceptable performance of either an individual team member or perhaps a single team among many that is not working productively in meeting the established goals. Addressing subpar performance issues with individual teachers is one of the most delicate responsibilities of the principal, and it is vital to fulfilling the responsibility of affirmation. Celebrating teacher performance that obviously aligns with our mission, vision, values, and goals, affirms their good work. However, when we confront underperformance of less stellar teachers, we once again affirm the behavior of our best teachers who notice and appreciate that such negative behaviors or subpar performance are considered unacceptable and are addressed by the principal as such.

To accomplish the delicate task of addressing teacher underperformance, we believe that such instances must be addressed with immediacy, built-in accountability structures, and supportive care. It is our responsibility to act on and not ignore failure when supporting evidence of such is brought to our attention or discerned. Therefore, we never hesitate to set up a face-to-face meeting with underperforming teachers to explicitly address the area(s) of concern. Based on the area of concern, we ask the teacher to provide appropriate referencing materials that might support or refute our concerns regarding their performance. We strive to meet with teachers in their classrooms to offer a level of comfort and ready access to any assisting materials and information; and perhaps most importantly, this makes other teachers, whether performing or not, aware that there are indeed swift consequences when failure ensues. Plus as previously mentioned, by directly addressing negative performance issues, the effective work of performing teachers is validated. While meeting, we sit beside the teacher and begin by asking, "How can we better support your efforts to accomplish (the goal of improving in the identified area)?" Then we listen intently. After providing uninterrupted attention, we express understanding where appropriate but make sure we relay with clarity that the issue is unacceptable and refer to attending material and evidence that supports our view. Moreover, we spend time problem solving, offering support, and developing support plans with desired outcome(s) together, never diminishing the issue nor allowing for inequality in relation to other teachers. Thereafter, we document the meeting by formally writing bulleted highlights of the discussion and issues addressed, forward it to the teacher to sign, provide a copy to the teacher, and keep a hardcopy in the teacher's files. Furthermore, we keep this issue at the forefront and purposely follow up through increased classroom observations with feedback, frequent collaborative review of the teacher's electronic grade book, close monitoring of peer collaboration, requests for progress artifacts and self-assessments, talks with students, assigned peer/team guidance, educational support, and more. If the teacher continues to underperform after the ascribed goal attainment date and exhausting all means of support, we seek separation for the good of student achievement and school prosperity. Ensuring that every classroom in the school is staffed by a highly effective teacher is our primary responsibility as instructional leaders. Therefore, we are relentless in addressing teacher underperformance, including, when appropriate, moving to terminate teachers unwilling or unable to perform to standards.

Another way we address underperforming teachers is through our three systematic, prescheduled professional learning meetings that are interconnected with our evaluation system conducted throughout the school year. Each teacher is assigned a *professional learning administrator,* either the principal or an assistant principal, and takes part in half-hour conversations centered around the individually created professional learning artifacts and with their *Content Collaboration Team* colleagues. For example, in the first meeting held in September, a self-assessment, team norms, and team SMART goals are due. At the second meeting held in December, a self-assessment, two peer observations, and a classroom walk-through are due. At the third meeting conducted in April, a self-assessment, professional reading and redelivery, common assessments, and student work analyses are due. Because evidence and accountability are inherent within each meeting, the opportunity to address underperformance is built in. While meeting, we listen, ask questions, and directly attend to both superior and inferior performance indicated through examination of the required artifacts, which by design encompass all aspects of teacher performance and responsibilities.

Responding When Students Do Not Learn

Although principals must address the issue of underperformance on the part of teachers, they must also lead the staff in answering the question, "How will we respond when students do not learn?" Once the school year begins, it takes very little time or effort to identify individual students in danger of failing. Although identifying such students is relatively simple, identifying ways to ensure high levels of learning for such students is anything but simple and requires the collective efforts of the entire school, led by the principal. One thing we have done to address the question of how we respond when kids do not learn is create and implement a school-wide *Pyramid of Interventions*. In recent years, many schools have adopted this practice of outlining, in hierarchical order, specific steps ensuring that all students learn and that the educators in the school do not give up on them. An example of such a systematic intervention strategy is included in the following text:

Otwell Middle School
Pyramid of Interventions for Student Achievement

The Otwell Middle School Pyramid of Interventions is the result of teamwork and collaboration. The catalyst for its development and implementation was the desire to have a common focus and a common language regarding instructional practices and interventions for meeting the individual needs of all students.

The Pyramid of Interventions provides a framework for aligning practices to fulfill our mission: "Our unrelenting quest is to do *Whatever It Takes* to teach, inspire and motivate all learners." This Pyramid of Interventions guides our school in responding to the following questions:

♦ Are all students learning?

♦ How do we know that they are learning?

♦ What are we doing when they do not learn?

We have learned that student growth is enhanced when assessment results are used to guide our continued instruction. By monitoring students' progress through daily assessments, we can determine if students are increasing their knowledge and skills as expected, or if additional instructional interventions are needed to ensure optimal academic success. The pyramid layers do not replace each other but build on each other, creating an individualized and systematic plan to answer the question, "What are we prepared to do when students do not learn?" The layers begin at the bottom (Level I) and work their way up, to Level VI, at which point the student is placed on a Student Support Team (SST) plan and perhaps even assessed for special education placement:

Level VI:

♦ SST Process Initiated

Level V:

♦ Academic Recovery Connections Program

Level IV:
- Chronic Academic Plan
- Working Connections
- On-Team Recovery
- In-School Suspension

Level III:
- Saturday Academy
- Small Group Counseling/Intentional Guidance

Level II:
- High School Mentors
- 8th Grade Peer Leaders Assist 6th and 7th Graders
- Administrative Recovery (morning work detention)
- Math Literacy Classes
- Reading Literacy Classes
- Instructional Extension Program
- SOS (Save One Student) Teacher Mentor Program

Level I:
- Connect Time: Connections Teachers Work With Students
- Collaboration With Support Teachers (ESOL, Special Ed, Gifted, Title I, Literacy)
- Voluntary Morning Tutoring
- Parent Volunteers
- Team Conference/Parent Conference
- Quality Work Designed
- Formative Assessments
- Differentiated Instruction

The schedule of previously listed interventions starts at the classroom level and moves up the pyramid to include specific interventions that the entire school community implements to ensure that all students are learning at high levels of performance. Each preceding intervention strategy was developed with the cooperation of the entire school staff and requires the collaboration and cooperation of all teachers across subject areas and grade levels. Like all schools committed to becoming and remaining true professional learning communities, we recognize the need to develop consistent systematic procedures that make certain each student at our school receives the time, support, and instruction necessary to succeed (DuFour, DuFour, Eaker, & Karhanek, 2004). The preceding specific intervention strategies are merely one faculty's example of steps they take to meet the needs of struggling students. It is not as important to go into detail regarding every step; it is important that each school principal lead the faculty and staff in a similar process that examines their own school community's current situation in terms of student learning and develops and implements their own specific strategies for intervening when students fail to learn.

Core Components

In reviewing aforementioned list of ideas, which suggest ways in which the school principal fulfills the leadership responsibility of *affirmation*, we determined that they fall into one or more of the following five categories, which seem to succinctly encapsulate what we see as the *core components* of this leadership responsibility:

Cornerstone #2: Affirmation

1. Actively Affirm:

Affirming principals realize it is the moral imperative of the principal to take purposeful steps forward, whether those steps be toward addressing achievement or failure.

2. Share the Stories:

Affirming principals regularly reveal individual and team accomplishments to ensure that imitation follows the art of success.

3. Provide Proof:

Affirming principals honor those committed to the core work and propel others to equally commit by following through on statements of purpose with tangible actions.

---

4.   Be Courageous:
Affirming principals face the fear of failure by facing those people and systems underperforming first.
5.   Choose Honesty:
Affirming principals realize that truthful conversations reveal indisputable facts—both brutal and laudable—and cultivate the capacity to act on them together.

The affirming leader plans for and responds to events during the day, which reveals this focus and exhibits a relentless quest to instill this focus in others within the school. The following illustration provides a brief snapshot of ways in which the principal affirms the efforts of all as she moves throughout her day:

A Glimpse of the Affirming Principal

"Mark Twain said he 'could live for two months on a good compliment,' and I believe him," composes Natalie Parker in her morning faculty e-mail. "And we are no different than Twain. So today, I encourage you to catch each other, including our students, performing well and let each other know." To start, Natalie adds that there are many recent accomplishments that she would like to recognize at Cornerstone High. Specifically, she reveals that Mr. Ben Byers and his marching band have been asked to perform in the All-State Band. In addition, the chemistry team of teachers has had an article accepted for publication in the *The Science Teacher* journal; and to honor their work, Natalie has purchased a year-long subscription to the journal to be added to Cornerstone's Professional Learning Community (PLC) library. Natalie also acknowledges that 83% of Cornerstone's senior fall applicants to the University of Georgia have been notified of their early acceptance. As a result Natalie thanks the entire faculty and notes that only a team working together toward a common goal ensures such a large acceptance and great accomplishment for students. Moreover, she extends a special congratulations to Susan Ericson and her ESOL department for acquiring and serving 16 new transfer ESOL students throughout this fall semester with ease and success, noting that most of these ESOL juniors passed the state-required writing test. Lastly, Natalie reminds the faculty of today's PLC meetings during each planning block, and encourages all to "Teach and learn with passion!"

As she concludes her e-mail and prints her day's calendar, Natalie promptly joins her team of assistant principals in the PLC conference room. While there, Natalie and her administrative team discuss the week in review and plan for the week ahead. In particular Jenna Smith, the assistant principal over the science and math departments, reports that the physical science content collaboration team has failed to meet their fall SMART (Specific, Measureable, Attainable, Results-Oriented, and Time-Bound) goals, because only 74% of the physical science students currently have a passing semester average going into the state-required End-of-Course test next week. Moreover, Jenna notes that Anna Klein has been absent from most bimonthly content collaboration meetings despite conversations and reminders otherwise. The team then discusses final plans for today's PLC with Natalie offering to facilitate all of first block and return for the recognition honors planned for every block thereafter.

Stephanie Walker, lead PLC facilitator, begins today's grading and reporting session promptly, and Natalie takes an active role as both participant and cofacilitator. Specifically, she closely monitors table talks and group work; and she asks questions to both individuals and teams as they discuss SMART goal assessment and attainment, especially the physical science team. Natalie advises that the team review Cornerstone's value statements and instructional *non-negotiables* as pedagogy may be at the heart of some student underperformance. Moreover, she directs the team to meet weekly during the coming spring semester, forward minutes with attendance records of each meeting, and let her know of meeting dates and times so she can attend to support and assist along the way. Natalie stresses her commitment to their teamwork and encourages SMART goal attainment next semester.

After rotating through the other content collaboration teams, Natalie learns of student achievement gains as a result of team-created common assessments. Natalie happily and publicly recognizes such achievements and SMART goal attainments during the latter part of the session. In addition, she reports that although most individual teams accomplished their SMART goals, collectively, the school did not reach their overarching SMART goal for decreasing student failures in core classes. As a result, next semester's PLC sessions focuses on exactly that and how refined Assessment for Learning practices can assist. Natalie reminds the faculty to be ongoing reflective educators and encourages each team to continue to ask hard questions of each other for the sake of optimal student and SMART goal achievement.

Thereafter and at the close of each PLC, Natalie hands out *Commendable Cougar* honors for an array of reasons. Today's honors are extended to content collaboration teams that met and exceeded fall SMART goals and individual teachers with the greatest student and class performance on common assessments. Each honoree receives a dinner for two from one of Cornerstone's Partners in Education.

With yesterday's class observation and today's physical science teamwork fresh on her mind, Natalie asks Anna Klein if she can walk to her classroom to follow up from yesterday's observation and discuss how she can best support Anna. While seated next to Anna, Natalie reviews all the positives found while observing Anna's fourth-block science class yesterday. In particular, Natalie commends Anna for the genuine care she offers and her positive rapport evident with each student interaction. Thereafter, Natalie asks Anna how she feels about the outcome of the lesson and student engagement throughout. Anna reveals that she feels "pretty good" about the lesson outcome, but she "wishes some of her students would take the work more seriously." Natalie listens intently, agrees, and offers some suggestions such as providing immediate academic feedback and using standards as a guide.

In addition, Natalie notes that she is aware of Anna's untimely grading and reporting. She reminds Anna of the school's instructional non-negotiables, including grading and reporting minimums, both of which Anna has failed to consistently uphold. Moreover, Natalie adds that Anna's collaborative responsibilities include meeting with her content collaboration teammates and emphasizes that her presence at team meetings is essential to honoring collective team and school commitments to the work and SMART goals for student achievement.

Lastly, Natalie invites Anna to seek assistance from her teammates, mentor, department chair, assistant principal, and her because greater support is needed and greater performance is expected. Anna apologizes for being remiss and acknowledges that she has been lacking follow through. Anna promises to seek out support as well. Natalie thanks Anna for her understanding and desire to grow as an educator and professional as she exists to class transitions.

While monitoring the commons area, she sees Sarah Carpenter, who invites Natalie to revisit her classes at any time, anxious to redeem herself after yesterday's "free day." Natalie plans to visit soon and thanks Sarah for being at her morning duty station without fail. Grateful that Natalie notices, Sarah smiles and heads to second block; and Natalie joins Stephanie in the PLC session underway.

At the beginning of third-block lunch, Natalie is approached by Anna Klein's mentor, Jill Stevens. Off to a side hall, Jill thanks Natalie for the honest conversation she had with Anna today, because Anna has already come to her seeking help. Natalie asks Jill to observe Anna's fourth-block class, if she hasn't already, and to share with Anna her class activity starters so the students get to work immediately upon entering class. Agreeing, Jill heads to lunch, and Natalie heads to third-block's PLC.

During the transition between third and fourth block, Natalie speaks to Robert Delatorre in the hall, asking him how he is doing in geometry. Listening to his tepid reply, she reveals that she noticed his unpreparedness and lack of focus in Ms. Klein's fourth-block physical science yesterday. Natalie tells Robert she expects him and every Cornerstone student to be prepared to learn every day and looks forward to witnessing a change in performance beginning today. Moreover, Natalie asks Robert to become a positive influence in the class, because she is aware of how much his peers seem to follow his lead. Robert promises to follow through on her requests.

When fourth block begins, Natalie lets Carla know she will be observing classes for most of fourth block, before taking part in the final recognition portion of PLC. She returns in time for afternoon announcements, encouraging each Cornerstone teacher and student to "extend your learning, yourself, and your heart."

Core Reflections

Consider the ideal *affirming* actions of Principal Parker and use the space provided to jot down examples of each core component found within this glimpse. Next, reflect on your own affirming leadership actions and include personal notes affirming your strengths and areas of needed growth.

Cornerstone #2: Affirmation

1. Actively Affirm:

2. Share the Stories:

3. Provide Proof:

4. Be Courageous:

5. Choose Honesty:

Personal Notes:

4

Ideal Beliefs

Cornerstone #3:

The school principal fulfills the responsibility of ideals/beliefs by possessing and sharing beliefs about education and by demonstrating behaviors consistent with those beliefs.

The third of nine leadership responsibilities identified by Marzano, Waters, and McNulty (2005), which fall directly under the purview of the school principal and ultimately relate to student achievement, is one the authors call *ideals/beliefs*. The authors stress the importance of this responsibility and call the development and cultivation of shared visions and ideals "intangible assets" of the school. Yet, they also caution, "Ideals/Beliefs might be one of the more difficult responsibilities for the school leader to execute" (p. 102). In analyzing seven quantitative research studies examining 513 schools related to this school leadership theme, the authors found an overall correlation of 0.22 between the leadership responsibility of ideals/beliefs and student academic achievement. Clearly, the entire school community must work together to discuss the specific beliefs, values, hopes, and dreams they have for their students and their schools and identify those core themes commonly held among most stakeholders. Ultimately, however, the school principal must initiate this discussion and lead the community in developing and publicizing written statements that convey the ideals and beliefs of the school.

The leadership responsibility of ideals/beliefs pervades every other leadership responsibility examined in this book. Its successful execution is necessary to optimize the efforts of all staff; affirm the performance of teachers, students, and the school as a whole; and effectively and efficiently manage the change process, an inevitable and annual challenge for school principals. Although developing mission, vision, value, and belief statements most directly falls under this leadership domain, we feel compelled to initiate its discussion in Chapter 1, because we consider it a vital part of serving as an optimizer. Perhaps no leadership responsibility is as critical to establishing a purposeful learning community as is the responsibility of ideals/beliefs. Discussing, debating, clarifying, writing, and displaying those ideals and beliefs about which we are passionate provide a *purpose* for the work we do in schools. Without formally undergoing an examination of our ideals and beliefs and identifying those that are commonly held, we are rudderless as a school and cannot move forward in targeting and achieving strategic goals for improved student learning.

The process of creating written documents that express the ideals and beliefs of the school community is a vital and necessary starting point for actually acting on those ideals and beliefs. This process has been examined at length in numerous books in recent years, so there is no need to revisit that process in any great detail here; but we do offer a brief version of our own views on what we want to create in terms of such documents and how we go about creating them. Suffice it to say that nearly all schools have adopted such statements, but only successful schools with strong leaders systematically and consistently follow through to ensure that those within the school are acting to align with the stated ideals. Before discussing the ways we act to make our ideal school a reality, we must decide the logistics of the process, beginning with the end product in mind: How will we phrase our statements of ideals and beliefs?

DuFour and Eaker (1998) make a compelling case for creating statements of mission, vision, values, and goals. Using this as our guide, we suggest establishing strong statements of mission, vision, and values, which are revisited every 3 to 5 years as a whole faculty. Principals new to a school should initiate this process as they begin their second year at a school, rather than arriving and immediately changing what is already in place. Goals, however, should be established annually and limited in number, with the entire school focusing on no more than five school-wide goals for improvement each year. The *mission* of the school succinctly states the purpose of the school, "its essential reason for educating, . . . expresses why a school *exists*" (Blankstein, 2004. p. 72). The *vision* of the school describes what we want to become and how we want to become known. It guides our actions as we strive to improve. Finally, the *values* we create should articulate the commitments we are willing to make to ensure that our mission is carried out each day and our vision becomes an enduring reality over time.

Senge (1990) maintains that without shared vision, we cannot achieve our goal of a true learning organization. A shared mission and shared values are equally important counterparts of strong schools. Again, although creating such statements is of paramount importance in establishing and communicating the ideals and beliefs of the school, it is merely a starting point and subordinate in importance to our subsequent actions. We must monitor our behaviors, eliminating those that are contrary to our stated beliefs and cultivating those that make our beliefs a reality. The principal who effectively fulfills the responsibility of ideals/beliefs does so in a variety of ways.

Following are just a few ways that principals can fulfill this responsibility as outlined in *School Leadership that Works*. (Marzano, et al., 2005). We begin by sharing one possible strategy for creating statements of mission, vision, and values and follow with ideas on how best to act on these by monitoring, communicating, and modeling actual behaviors. These suggestions are described in some detail and then followed by a brief list of five thoughts summarizing our experiences in this critical area.

Ideals/Beliefs: Points to Ponder

Creating Statements of belief

A school cannot begin to live out its mission, achieve its vision, or act in accordance to its values until, of course, these statements are created. Again, nearly every school in recent years has either created or revised some type of public document relating to its mission, vision, and values making a lengthy examination of the process unnecessary here. Yet, the importance of engaging the school community in this undertaking cannot be overstated. These statements must be crafted with a purpose and should guide the school in deciding on its direction. These statements help us decide what to do and what to *stop* doing. Once the statements are crafted and adopted, decisions must be made with these statements in mind. We should not discuss whether to implement a new initiative without first asking, "Will it help us fulfill our mission?" If an activity does not contribute to the school's mission, don't do it.

At one of our schools, we worked to revise the statements that were already in place when we arrived, moving from a mission statement supported with statements of beliefs to statements of mission, vision, and values. We took our time on this process and worked to educate the entire school community on the importance of each aspect of such a belief system. We stressed that these should serve as the foundation of a professional learning community (DuFour and Eaker, 1998) and that they should answer three simple, yet specific, questions:

1. Mission: *Why* do we exist?
2. Vision: *What* do we hope to become?
3. Values: *How* will we make our shared vision a reality?

At our school, one thing we all seem to value is humor, so after explaining the entire purpose and prior to actually brainstorming ideas for our new mission, vision, and values, we shared a PowerPoint slideshow titled, "Top Ten Rejected Mission Statements." These were a fun way to begin what can otherwise become a tedious undertaking for many teachers already jaded by talk of mission statements. A few of our facetious top ten mission statements included the following:

- ◆ "Because We're A School of Excellence, That's Why."
- ◆ "No Behind Left on a Child."
- ◆ "Using SST, IEP, and SEPC to examine GHSGT, MGWA, CRCT, and ITBS through our PLCs and PACs so that we can kick BUTT."
- ◆ "We engineer innovative education while using an inquiry-centered curriculum to mesh cross-curricular learning and optimize site-based enrichment. Students become lifelong learners as they realize student-centered learning outcomes while absorbing standards-based instructional practices."

After laughing at ourselves in this way, we enjoyed one more frivolous icebreaker before turning to our real work: we showed a 5-minute clip from the popular Tom Cruise movie *Jerry Maguire* in which the famous sports agent has a vision in the middle of the night, which he writes in a frenzy, prints for the entire organization, and places in each employee's mailbox. The fact that this leads to his temporary fall from grace within the organization was another fun way to begin our own process of creating a mission, vision, and values.

After this, we dedicated one professional development day to creating each of our three core statements. Our process was simple and not unlike what many other schools have likely followed. We divided the faculty into groups of 10, making sure to mix each group with members from various departments and assigning a respected teacher leader as the group facilitator. Then, we followed a simple 10-step plan for brainstorming ideas.

1. Give each person an index card.
2. Tell the group to write *one* item they believe must be included in the school mission statement. Don't get hung up on exact wording, and avoid clichés.
3. Turn in index card to facilitator.
4. Facilitator shuffles cards and redistributes them.
5. Each person reads the card they have, as facilitator lists them on large chart paper.
6. Any cards that are similar are combined, and the originals crossed out.
7. Facilitator gives each person five adhesive dots.

8. Each person puts a dot next to the five statements they feel are the most important (may use more than one dot per item if they feel strongly about it).

9. Copy the top 10 statements in order of importance (listing the statement with the most dots first, etc.) on the other piece of chart paper.

10. Post the list in the Media Center.

Once we returned to the Media Center as a whole faculty, we *gallery walked* through each group's list and developed a list of five core themes we saw emerging. Then we solicited volunteers to serve on a writing committee to put these themes into a succinct statement. Although we started with the mission statement, we followed a similar statement for creating a vision and list of core values. After all three were complete, we shared them with the entire faculty, our Parent Teacher Organization, our Local School Council, and all parents and students before formally adopting them as our new statements that would guide our actions as educators.

Once we create such documents, they should be used to motivate teachers. It is much easier for teachers to work hard if they feel that they are contributing to something important, something bigger. We try to make everyone feel connected to the work we do and have spelled out carefully in our public declarations. Although these documents can motivate our highest performing teachers, they can also serve to motivate our underperforming teachers to either improve or move on. Not long after we adopted our own statements stressing our core values as a school community, one of our least effective teachers decided to resign because she no longer felt comfortable working in an environment in which almost every other teacher was committed to our mission, vision, and values.

Promoting Beliefs Through Words and Actions

Once we craft and adopt statements that communicate our shared ideals and beliefs, we must publicize them in a variety of ways to keep them in the forefront of our minds. We do this in several ways. First, each Monday, we send out an e-mail that we call, "Thank God, It's Monday," which communicates the week's events among other things. To start each Monday memo, we include, in large bold letters, either our mission, our vision, or one of our five value statements. We also made attractive laminated placards for each of our three core statements and posted these in a prominent position within every room in the building. In addition, we include our statements in our monthly newsletter to parents and community members. We incorporate our mission, vision, and values into the awards we present each other, often considering to what extent a person is fulfilling our commonly held ideals and beliefs before recognizing them with a significant honor like Teacher of the Year or induction into our Teaching Hall of Fame.

Each fall we distribute student handbooks to all students. This is another opportunity we seize to communicate our statements of mission, vision, and values to our students and their parents. Each morning before our video announcements begin, we scroll our statements of ideals and beliefs on the screens of our classroom televisions. In addition, we also display our mission, vision, and values statements prominently on our school's web site. Finally, at whole faculty meetings, we often try to remind our teachers of our purpose, our hopes, and our commitments to making these a reality. We announce specific actions or accomplishments that have occurred and have advanced our mission, vision, or values. Too often, in our experience, schools exert considerable energy and dedicate much time to developing statements of ideals and beliefs only to forget them after a brief period of time. As principals, we must give teachers daily reminders of our purpose for educating and how we can accomplish our purpose.

Although creating statements of ideals and beliefs and communicating these through many different avenues is extremely important, it is even more critical that we promote our ideals and beliefs through our actions. In our school, the words, "whatever it takes" are included in our mission. Although this is a popular catchphrase in education today, at our school it has become a vital component of our learning culture. Whenever a student is not learning, we remind ourselves that we have committed to doing "whatever it takes" to ensure that he does learn. Depending on the situation, this may mean that we work before or after school or even on Saturdays providing remediation. It may mean, as it has in our school, that all school administrators and counselors teach classes regularly in core areas for students who need extra support. It may mean that we refuse to allow our students off the hook by assigning grades of *zero*. Instead, we hold them accountable for their learning by insisting that they complete the missing or incomplete assignment. Similarly, we may offer second-chance opportunities for learning if students fail a test or quiz, allowing them to retake the assessment at a later date to show that they have worked to learn the intended outcomes.

In our school's vision, we state that we will excel in all areas, including community involvement. Here, too, our actions must align with our words. If community involvement is important enough to include in our statement of vision, we must hold each other accountable for ensuring that we act to make it a reality. At our school, both students and staff are involved in numerous activities throughout the year that help our surrounding community. Through our clubs and organizations, our students assist at senior citizen events, including singing Christmas carols during the holidays. We also conduct an annual food drive during Thanksgiving to help those in need; and we host an International Night, inviting community members of diverse backgrounds to enjoy a meal and take home clothing items we have collected to give away. As a school, we respond whenever tragedy strikes, such as Hurricane Katrina, by collecting and sending as many needed resources as we can, and we participate in aluminum and paper recycling efforts throughout the school year. As a staff, we regularly lead all schools in our district in money donated to cancer research through our Relay for Life campaign and we also contribute significantly to United Way. More importantly, we volunteer our time as we work with our students to assist others in our community and beyond who need our help.

Promoting Positive Classroom Behaviors

One of our value statements suggests that we will promote and insist on a safe and orderly learning environment. As principals, we play a key role in supporting this value and making certain that each staff member at our school is equally committed to it. To begin with, we must communicate what we believe constitutes a *safe and orderly* school and how we best go about achieving it. We are fervent believers that the best discipline plan in the classroom is an outstanding lesson plan, yet we know that even our best teachers encounter student behavior challenges periodically. We typically share the following list of statements relating to classroom management for teachers to reflect on as we begin each new school year, asking them to rank each statement from 1 to 4, ranging from *almost always* to *almost never*:

_____ 1. I am friendly but firm with my students.

_____ 2. I treat each student with kindness and respect.

_____ 3. When a student or students act inappropriately, I remain calm and composed.

_____ 4. I display enthusiasm and a sense of humor with my students.

_____ 5. During each passing period between classes, I am at the doorway to greet and chat with students.

_____ 6. I insist that students treat me with dignity and respect.

_____ 7. I interact with all students, not just a few.

_____ 8. I give my students a pleasing greeting each day and wish them a pleasant weekend.

_____ 9. During each passing period between classes, I am at the doorway so I can supervise both the hallway and my classroom.

_____ 10. So that I know what is going on in my classroom, I generally spend my class time on my feet.

_____ 11. I expect students to listen attentively when another student or I am talking.

_____ 12. When I correct student misbehavior, I communicate in a private, positive, and respectful manner.

_____ 13. I admit that at times student misbehavior is a result of something that was my fault.

_____ 14. I am able to motivate my students, including the reluctant learner.

_____ 15. I carefully plan each lesson so that there is no dead time.

_____ 16. I provide guided or independent practice during which I move about the room offering individual or small-group assistance.

_____ 17. During each class period, I provide a variety of learning activities. Rarely do I use an entire period for a single activity, because students need a change of pace.

_____ 18. I adjust my daily lesson planning to take into account my students' span of attention.

_____ 19. I think through discipline decisions before acting.

_____ 20. I make only those discipline decisions that I can enforce.

_____ 21. I make discipline decisions after the heat of the moment has passed.

_____ 22. When a student misbehaves in class, I find a way to correct the behavior privately, perhaps by moving near the student and whispering a correction.

_____ 23. While I take attendance or perform other necessary tasks, often at the outset of each class session, my students are working independently, perhaps on a brief assignment or problem on the overhead or board.

_____ 24. I establish time-saving routines for collecting papers and distributing materials or supplies.

_____ 25. My directions for a learning activity are brief and concise.

_____ 26. I give directions one step at a time. I avoid long and detailed directions.

_____ 27. I show sincere enthusiasm for the subjects I teach.

_____ 28. I provide a neat classroom that gives students the idea of orderliness.

_____ 29. I present a professional appearance in the classroom.

_____ 30. I insist that my students maintain high standards in their work and behavior. In both areas, my standards are realistic and attainable.

_____ 31. Because there is no best teaching method, my methods and learning activities are many and varied.

_____ 32. My homework assignments have a purpose, are instructional, and are regulated as to the time it will take a student to complete the assignment.

_____ 33. I make my classroom attractive by having effective bulletin boards related to the topics studied at the particular time.

_____ 34. During each class session, I summarize, or have students summarize, the day's learning.

_____ 35. I use pretests or other procedures to ascertain what students already know.

The preceding statements accomplish several purposes. Of course, we hope they help teachers ruminate on their own practices relating to classroom management, yet we also realize that they are a powerful way of conveying some of our own core ideals and beliefs in this critical area of our school.

In addition to sharing our beliefs about classroom management issues as we do through the preceding statements, we are highly visible at all times, walking in the halls, cafeterias, and common areas as well as visiting classes every day. We also insist that teachers remain vigilant about this. Like many schools, most of our discipline incidents occur outside the classroom walls. It is imperative, therefore, that all teachers are visible in the hallways during transition times. Finally, we are firm, fair, and consistent in dealing with discipline referrals written by teachers. Although we require a great deal from our teachers in this area and hold clear expectations that they communicate with parents and take other proactive steps in dealing with student misbehavior, once a referral is turned in to administration, it is *always* dealt with swiftly, and a consequence of some sort is meted out. Of course, if we note that a certain teacher is writing an excessive number of referrals or writing frivolous referrals, we confront that situation on an individual basis; but most teachers at our schools send very few, if any, discipline referrals to the office. When they do, our commitment as administrators is to immediately deal with and resolve the incident. Although we are always fair to our students, we also want to make our teachers feel supported as they follow through on one of our key stated values.

The preceding scenarios describe just a few ways in which we act to uphold our mission, our vision, and our values. This is a commitment we must adhere to on a daily basis through the actions we take and the decisions we make. Actions and decisions alike must support our purpose, our dreams, and our stated commitments.

Using Beliefs to Effect Change

Obviously, we strongly support the idea that principals should lead their faculty in a school wide effort to discuss, debate, and create shared ideals and beliefs to identify commonalities they hold regarding the nature and purpose of education. At the same time, we want each individual teacher to feel free to act in a way that builds off their unique strengths and personality. Although our very best teachers support and work to fulfill the mission of the school, not all of them possess identical skill sets. We must honor individual differences among our teachers while at the same time adhering to our shared ideals. In an effort to encourage teachers to consider their own philosophy of schooling, we ask each teacher to create their own professional mission statement and display this in their classroom and on their teacher web page. Many teachers take pride in crafting these statements of purpose and include inspirational quotes that motivate them as teachers and as lifelong learners.

The most important by-product of having explicit statements of mission, vision, and values in place and communicating these beliefs consistently and effectively occurs when it becomes obvious—through a careful examination of data—that change is necessary in some area of the school to improve performance. Like most principals, we have been faced with such situations on numerous occasions. In these situations, it is vitally important that we rely on our commonly shared beliefs as we look to implement change. This recently occurred at one of our schools when we were forced to confront the brutal fact that student math achievement was significantly below what we expected and unacceptable when compared to results achieved at schools with similar demographics. Ultimately, we carved out a 30-minute block of time during the school day for every certified staff member—including administrators—to teach fundamental math skills to a small group of students. This time was used to reinforce concepts learned during regular math classes. Needless to say, this innovation was met with a fair amount of resistance, especially at first, as we worked to convince art, music, physical education, and language arts teachers that they needed to spend 30 minutes each day teaching math. Part of our success in getting everyone to accept this idea was our insistence that we adhere to our mission of doing *whatever it takes* to help our students learn. In this particular situation, students were only receiving math instruction every other day for 90 minutes; based on test results as well as expert opinions (from our math teachers), we determined that we had to find a way to increase the amount of time spent teaching and learning math every day. After a year of this extra *mini* math period each day, our standardized test scores in math increased dramatically from the previous year, earning our school statewide recognition for highest gains in math achievement.

Not every teacher at our school was overjoyed by this change in their daily routine, but an increasing number of teachers became excited as they saw what we were accomplishing through our collective efforts. A key to our success was enlisting the help of every certified staff member and explaining that we had to act in a swift and decisive manner because our stated beliefs compelled us to accept nothing less than high levels of learning for all students.

Both Laura Link and I consider Roland Barth one of our educational heroes. Barth is well known for suggesting that a leader makes happen what he or she believes in (1990). Although we had both read Barth's words years before and noted their inherent wisdom, it was not until my third year as principal that I—after attending a conference at which Barth spoke—returned to our school determined to find out if the teachers at our school really knew what *I* believed in most fervently. Standing in front of our faculty, I paraphrased Barth's quote about what makes a leader and first asked teachers to share what they believed in and what they worked hardest at to make happen in their classrooms. The responses were immediate and powerful as teachers began sharing their personal passions. I followed this by asking teachers to discern my own most passionate belief about leading our school, based on their observations of my actions. One teacher started things off and elicited a laugh by suggesting, "Better pay for all teachers?" This was quickly followed by several thoughtful and gratifying suggestions, all of which were indeed core beliefs of mine. The third or fourth hand that went up was that of a veteran teacher who I consider one of our very best teacher leaders. She stated confidently, "Building positive relationships," which made my day. Like all dedicated educators, I hold many core beliefs and strive to make many things happen at our school. Forced to choose only one, I would have echoed the words that this respected teacher had identified as my core passion. Standing in front of your faculty and inviting them to guess what you most believe in can be a bit nerve wracking, as you anxiously wonder if teachers have surmised from your actions your core beliefs about teaching and learning. It is also a powerful way to get teachers thinking again about what we all want to make happen in our schools, individually and collectively. Robbins and Alvy (2004) suggest that new principals stand in front of their faculty at their first faculty meeting and state their vision about schooling. We concur and suggest that this is an activity worth engaging in at least once each year thereafter.

Core Components

In reviewing the previous list of ideas that suggest ways for the school principal to fulfill the leadership responsibility of *ideals/beliefs,* we determined that they fall into one or more of the following five categories, which seem to succinctly encapsulate what we see as the core components of this leadership responsibility:

Cornerstone #3: Ideals/Beliefs
1. Set Your Anchor: Beliefs-focused principals commit to a set of ideals and beliefs and hold steadfast to their execution despite waves of dissent and drifts from their center.
2. Shape Your Course: Beliefs-focused principals use shared ideals/beliefs as a regular and consistent guide to navigate next steps, make decisions, enact change, and refine actions.
3. Market to All: Beliefs-focused principals reinforce and enlist commitment to shared ideals/beliefs by publicizing them to all school stakeholders in a variety of ways and venues.
4. Model the Ideal: Beliefs-focused principals regularly demonstrate and enliven the school's ideals/beliefs through both purposeful and unplanned actions.
5. Mirror the Mission: Beliefs-focused principals realize that the school's ideals/beliefs must be a reflection of all those working to achieve them. Otherwise, they hold no power to effect change.

The beliefs-focused leader plans for and responds to events during the day, which reveals this focus and exhibits a relentless quest to instill this focus in others within the school. The following illustration provides a brief snapshot of ways the principal conveys her beliefs and acts accordingly as she moves throughout her day.

A Glimpse of the Beliefs-Focused Principal

"As we face our few remaining learning opportunities we have with students this semester," composes Natalie Parker with conviction, "I am reminded of a poignant quote by Peter Elbow that should be at the forefront as we communicate and make final decisions about learning that has taken place in our care. According to Elbow (1986), through sound assessment practices, 'we can tell a little more of the truth. In doing so, it turns out that we can avoid pretending that a student's whole performance or intelligence can be summed up in one number.' Although we are ultimately obligated to quantify learning, I ask each of you to reflect on our shared assessment beliefs when addressing evaluations and reporting final grades to ensure that (1) students have been given multiple opportunities to learn; (2) students have been provided regular and consistent feedback for the purpose of improvement; (3) students have been enabled to actively participate in the discovery process and evaluate their own learning; (4) evidence of student learning has been collected, organized, and presented over time." Natalie closes her weekly e-mail by thanking the faculty for upholding the school's mission this semester because she has witnessed many instances where teachers have done *whatever it takes* to ensure student success. Specifically, she notes Aaron Bell's after school and Saturday morning geometry sessions held for any student seeking extra geometry lessons in preparation for the End-of-Course test, Ben Byers' peer tutoring sessions held the first 20 minutes of each marching band practice, Henry Gill's precision with multifarious balanced assessments, Susan Ericson's intensive student writing workshops, Rafael Santiago's late-night media center hours of operation, and Harvey Nichols' maintenance of a spotless learning environment every day. She concludes by reminding all Advanced Studies teachers of today's *Lunch and Learn* and asks for each teacher's list of students "at-risk" of failing any course this semester, including documentation of parental communication and a sampling of student work and assessments, by the close of the week. Lastly, Natalie encourages everyone to "enlist evidence" before evaluating and "teach and learn with passion" to accomplish.

Before first block, Natalie monitors transition and notes the updated common's bulletin board that includes Cornerstone's ever-present mission, vision, and value statements within, then heads to her planned Parent Academy meeting.

Approximately 20 parents greet Natalie as she smiles, shakes hands, and passes out the day's agenda framed with Cornerstone's assessment belief statements. Co-facilitating the meeting, Natalie and her Parent-Teacher Student Organization President, Liz Franklin, thank all participants for attending and review the assessment for learning focus of today's meeting. The group, comprised of any teacher who has first-block planning (rotating to a different planning block each month) and any interested Cornerstone High School parent, meets to discuss and inform current school practices. Yet, before discussion, a close reading of the school's value statements ensues; these values are used as guiding principles throughout the conversation. Today's focus, "Communicating About Learning," stirs positive discussion about what constitutes demonstration of learning and how parents can and should respond to their child's learning. Jill Stevens, a teacher in attendance, assures the group that she is responsible for delivering a summary of today's meeting to the faculty, and Liz Franklin offers to post a summary of outcomes on the school's web page under "Beliefs in Practice."

Grateful for another meaningful home/school discussion, Natalie passes through the counseling suite after second block begins. As she walks by Joanna Price's counseling office, she asks if "everything is okay," noting that a student in Joanna's care is clearly distressed. After further inquiry, Natalie learns that the senior student, Rachel Riles, is at great risk of failing two classes and not graduating on time as a result of depression stemming from her parent's recent divorce and added financial strains. Pleased with Ms. Price's response to assist thus far, Natalie works with Joanna to secure teachers to tutor Rachel during her lunch every day and for Rachel to attend study skills and test prep sessions facilitated by Cornerstone's graduation coach every afternoon. Moreover, Natalie speaks with Rachel's mother to collaborate their shared plans and learning goals. Thereafter, Natalie offers a class ring, at her expense, if Rachel meets all goals, including graduating on time.

Hopeful that Rachel will achieve, Natalie heads to her office and reviews two at-risk student files of the many that Anna Klein, Robert Delatorre's physical science teacher, handed in. Not surprised that Robert was one of the students of concern, Natalie calls Robert's father, Mr. Delatorre, to review Cornerstone's non-negotiable intervention practices that will require serious commitment from all stakeholders.

Pleased with Mr. Delatorre's response and appreciation for the planned interventions, Natalie exits Cornerstone's main building under a large, scrolling digital sign that decrees, "Through these doors walk the finest people in the world: our students, their parents, our faculty, and our guests." From there, Natalie joins her Advanced Studies teachers for a working lunch to finalize Cornerstone's summer reading policy in their advanced placement (AP) and international baccalaureate (IB) programs.

Facilitating the meeting, Jill Stevens provides an overview from today's Parent Academy and reminds the committee to take all stakeholder input into consideration as they make decisions today. Thereafter, Jill reviews Cornerstone's mission and value statements, especially noting the assessment statements that reside prominently and permanently on the Professional Learning Community's walls. Next, Jill reminds that after surveying students, parents, and other Cornerstone teachers throughout the fall, the task at hand is to either amend or keep the current summer reading policy, which has been hotly debated throughout the semester. The current policy requires interested students to complete multiple reading assignments, projects, and written papers the summer prior to entering AP or IB courses. Moreover, major assessments over this summer work are occurring the first few days of students entering classes.

And today the committee is charged with ensuring that the reading decision upholds the school's mission: "Caring for all by doing whatever it takes to maximize learning opportunities for every Cornerstone student every day." And with this mission in mind, the committee concluded, although without unanimity, that the current summer reading policy must be amended and perhaps even changed completely. Under the current summer practices, students are not provided with multiple opportunities to learn, necessary feedback on performance, and evidence that learning has taken place before the evaluations on the first few days of classes. Most importantly, with the sheer quantity of summer assignments, combined with inadequate assessment practices, the current policy is excluding students that may otherwise take part under collaborative and fair practices—all counter to Cornerstone's mission.

Natalie thanks the committee for their good work and poses two questions: (1) What would summer reading would look like and entail if it upheld the school's mission and beliefs? (2) What is the purpose of summer reading and how will we ensure that we are accomplishing this purpose?

Reflecting on her own answers to the posed questions, Natalie monitors the lunchrooms before observing in classrooms for the remainder of third block.

After witnessing wonderful lessons, Natalie joins two of her assistant principals, Andrew Sutton and Jenna Smith, to privately discuss recent teacher observations and review electronic grade books of teachers who may be inconsistently upholding the school's non-negotiable grading/reporting practices and assessment beliefs in particular. Not surprisingly, both Anna Klein and Sarah Carpenter come up in conversation, because both assistant principals have also witnessed very limited assessment for learning practices, and parents are upset that they are not seeing timely grading and reporting in either class. In addition, a review of their grade books reveals many zeros assigned for student work and many students failing their classes. Natalie shares her conversation and concerns already addressed with Anna Klein just yesterday, and indicates that she will arrange to meet with Sarah Carpenter the next day to review similar concerns.

Thereafter, Natalie thanks Andrew and Jenna and returns to her office to make the afternoon announcements, encouraging each Cornerstone teacher and student to "extend your learning, yourself, and your heart."

Core Reflections

Consider the ideal *belief-focused* actions of Principal Parker and use the space provided to jot down examples of each core component found within this glimpse. Next, reflect on your own beliefs-focused leadership actions and include personal notes affirming your strengths and areas of needed growth.

Cornerstone #3: Ideals/Beliefs

1.   Set Your Anchor:

2.   Shape Your Course:

3.   Market to All:

4.   Model the Ideal:

5.   Mirror the Mission:

Personal Notes:

5

Awareness

Cornerstone #4:

The school principal fulfills the responsibility of situational awareness by staying alert to the positive and negative interactions, events, and undercurrents in the school and using this knowledge to anticipate and prevent potential problems.

The fourth of nine leadership responsibilities identified by Marzano, Waters, and McNulty (2005), which fall directly under the purview of the school principal and ultimately relate to student achievement, is one the authors call, *situational awareness.* Having awareness of all that occurs within the school is closely related to the leadership responsibility discussed in the Chapter 6, Visibility. Effective execution of the latter makes effective communication of the former all the more likely. As the authors suggest, it intuitively makes sense that principals who are aware of all that occurs in the school are more likely to be successful leaders. Yet, all too often, overwhelmed by the various demands of the job, principals are unaware of subtle signs that potential problems are brewing among teachers, students, or parents. Fulfilling this responsibility lessens the likelihood that a principal is surprised by a seemingly sudden crisis. Moreover, fulfilling this responsibility has been found to correlate to student academic achievement. As a matter of fact, the responsibility of situational awareness has the largest correlation to student achievement of all 21 responsibilities examined in *School Leadership that Works* (Marzano, et al., 2005). In analyzing five quantitative research studies examining 91 schools related to this school leadership theme, the authors found an overall correlation of 0.33 between the leadership responsibility of situational awareness and student academic achievement. Armed with this information, principals at strong schools make it a priority to remain intimately aware of all that occurs within the schools they lead.

In examining research-based classroom management strategies, Marzano, Marzano, and Pickering (2003) found that teachers with effective classroom management skills approach their classrooms with a specific mental set, which includes being aware of every student in the classroom and anticipating potential behaviors which might disrupt the learning environment. The authors state that effective classroom managers are skilled in the area of what they call "withitness", that is, "the ability to identify and quickly act on potential behavior problems" (p. 65). They offer three strategies for increasing one's ability to cultivate withitness: react immediately, forecast problems, and observe a master teacher. School leaders must also identify potential problems within the school and act quickly to resolve them. In this aspect of education, the classroom is a microcosm for the entire school. Although teachers must be keenly aware of all that is overtly and subtly occurring within their classrooms, the principal must accomplish this on a school-wide basis, monitoring and responding to the inner workings of the school as perceived by staff, students, and community.

The principal who effectively fulfills the responsibility of situational awareness does so in a variety of ways. Following are just a few ways that principals can fulfill this responsibility as outlined in *School Leadership that Works* (Marzano, et al., 2005). These suggestions are described in some detail and then followed by a brief list of five thoughts summing up our experiences in this critical area.

Situational Awareness: Points to Ponder

Principal Visibility

Although our primary focus in identifying ways in which to fulfill the responsibility of situational awareness relates to being aware of the status of the school as perceived by teachers, it is also important that the principal is aware of student and parent perceptions regarding the functioning of the school. In Chapter 6 we examine in more detail principal visibility, but it merits consideration here, too, as the single most practical way for the principal to become and remain aware of student, parent, and teacher perceptions. One way we remain visible to students and aware of what they are thinking is extremely simple and something almost any school official would agree is best practice: Each and every day, the principal stands in front of the school greeting and shaking the hand of every student arriving at school by car. At the same time, we station an assistant principal at our other entrance, where bus riding students arrive. She greets and shakes the hand of every student arriving by bus. We do this for 30 minutes every morning, 180 days out of 180 days. Nothing we do is as effective as this simple practice in terms of getting to know our students: who they are, what they look like, how they are dressed, the moods they are in, the attitudes they possess, and most importantly the insights they have into how we are doing as a school.

Although nearly all would agree that this is a solid recommendation for school administrators, we have found that this practice is the exception, rather than the rule, among principals. We *know* we should do this, but we often fail to *do* it. We face a multitude of obstacles keeping us from doing this, of course. The morning time is prime time for meetings of every variety. It is a fine time to catch up on e-mails or phone messages. We get called away to meetings at the central office. The student population increases to the point that we feel we cannot do this in a school with 2,000 or more students. Despite all these obstacles, we consider this—as Covey (1989) suggests—not merely a "have to" for principals, but a "must do." We accomplish this by also recalling his advice to put our first things first. Student arrival occurs first thing each morning and we consider greeting them our first and foremost responsibility each morning. On the rare occasions when we simply cannot follow through on this priority ourselves, we make sure that we secure a *substitute* staff member to fill in for us.

Although we have found this to be a great public relations practice with the entire community as well as a lot of fun, our primary purpose is to become fully aware of our students. Through this simple practice, carried out consistently over time, we have managed to memorize the names of a huge percentage of our students, even at extremely large high schools. The more familiar we become with these students, the more we learn about them—and from them. As they begin to rely on our daily presence, they also begin to let us know their thoughts about our school. Nary has a day passed without us learning something that makes us more alert to occurrences within our school. I am writing these words on a Friday in January. This week, in the car rider line, one student told me that we are doing a good job of preventing bullying at our school. Another told me that we need a daily "study hall" at our school. Several have asked me if I am going to our home basketball games tonight. Still others have predicted that I am sure to be defeated in the three-point shooting contest during our afternoon pep rally (they also demand to know why we cannot have more pep rallies). A handful of parents have made a point of rolling down their car windows and complimenting me on the awards ceremonies we held this week to recognize students for first-semester academic excellence. One student came carrying my weekly morning doughnut, like she has done every Friday for the past 2 years! And on Monday, a mother of another student pulls off to the side with a crying eighth-grade daughter in her truck. She tells me that her daughter refuses to come to school. Although I know this student well, I am unsuccessful in my attempts to cajole her into getting out of the truck. Finally, I call one of her teachers to save the day. We get an assistant principal to cover this teacher's class while the teacher spends the first hour of the day meeting privately with this student, listening to her story, and planning how we can work to resolve the conflicts in her life.

Meanwhile, at the bus arrival area this week, we are made aware of two potential student fights because of our presence. One situation was reported to our assistant principal by several students and another was reported by a bus driver. Another student has informed us that one of our eighth-grade girls has tobacco in her purse. A group of students on another bus informs us that the new bus driver is taking a slightly different route than the previous driver, which is making them arrive too late to eat breakfast at school. These are among the many things that we learned from our students in just 1 week, simply because we are there each day. As we suggest in the following chapter, we cannot be *aware* if we are not *there*.

Parent and Student Advisory Councils

Another way we work to become more aware of student and parent perceptions of how our school is functioning is through our parent and student advisory committees. Many years ago, our superintendent of schools established Student Advisory (SAC), Teacher Advisory (TAC), and Parent Advisory (PAC) committees. These committees include representative members of each stakeholder group from across the system, and they meet quarterly to discuss the direction of the system as a whole. We perceived this to be an effective practice and thought it might be even more effective at a site-based level, so we established our own SAC and PAC. Our SAC is made up of three students from each grade level who are selected by teachers as possessing the leadership qualities necessary to represent the views of the entire student body and being able to communicate these to the principal. We meet bimonthly for lunch, discussing issues of concern in the eyes of our students. Inevitably, we have discussed dress code issues and the quality of our cafeteria food. We have also, however, worked together to improve our school in subtle but important ways. Working on the SAC, students devised a much more logical way to assign lockers, based on grade level and location of classes. Another year, the SAC worked to create a list of five *Student Value Statements* similar to our faculty value statements. These statements outlined five actions to which all students in the school should commit themselves. The SAC also worked with the principal to provide some consistency to the amount of homework assigned, so that students were not overwhelmed with homework and/or tests on any single day of the week.

We organize our PAC in a slightly different manner. Rather than elect a fixed number of parents to this council each year, we simply host monthly *Coffee with the Principal* gatherings in our cafeteria. These are typically held from 9:00 a.m. to 10:00 a.m., after students have finished breakfast and before they return for lunch. The meetings are advertised on our marquee and in our monthly newsletter. All parents are invited to attend and share concerns or ideas they might have and to hear news from the principal regarding the status of the school. We typically have between 20 and 30 parents in attendance each month since the program's inception. Like the SAC, the work of the PAC has produced several tangible benefits. For example, several parents who are regular PAC participants organized a *Helping Hands* parent volunteer program. These parents volunteered to tutor students during the school day on a regular basis at the elementary school level and even at the middle school level. They felt that there was still a need for such academic support at the high school level. These PAC participants worked to target a handful of willing parents who possessed the academic content expertise necessary to remediate instruction and mentor a small group of students identified as ones who might benefit from this extra assistance.

By implementing SAC and PAC and actively seeking their input about how the school is functioning, we feel we have a greater awareness of what is working well in addition to what we need to examine a bit more carefully. The key to success in our own student and parent programs has been our willingness to listen as much as we talk. We treat these forums as genuine opportunities to hear from our customers and learn how we can improve. In a short period of time, both organizations have produced work that has raised our awareness of how we are doing and helped us prevent potential problems.

Soliciting Teacher Feedback

As important as it is to gain and maintain a thorough awareness of how parents and students perceive the functioning of the school, it is even more important that principals cultivate this awareness from the perspective of teachers. An informal way we do this each day is by sitting with teachers during lunch periods. Many principals are so busy during midday that they eat a hurried lunch at their desk while completing important tasks, or forego lunch altogether. Although we are not big lunch eaters ourselves, we make it a daily habit to join a group of teachers while they eat lunch. It is important to join different groups throughout the year and not eat with the same group of teachers every day. We have found that investing 20 or 30 minutes of our time each day to sitting with teachers as they enjoy lunch together provides us the opportunity to learn a great deal about teachers and how they perceive what is occurring with the school. This practice has made us much more aware of situations involving our teachers, their students, and the events occurring in their classrooms that affect academic achievement. We have been able to anticipate problems before they arise and act to prevent them from interfering with student learning.

Another way that we attempt to become more aware of situations occurring within our school is by gleaning insights from our teachers through the use of anonymous surveys. We have used various staff surveys over the years for a variety of purposes. At times, we are trying to gauge how we are doing in a particular area of the school, such as discipline, the school schedule, or school safety. More often, we are simply trying to get teachers to respond to open ended questions, such as, "How can we improve our school?" or "What can the school administrators do to help teachers teach and students learn?" Typically, we tend to survey our teachers in this general way near the close of each semester. We have also mailed surveys home to teachers during the summer, asking them to reflect on the school year just completed and offer suggestions as we plan for the one about to begin.

Regardless of the types of surveys we create, we are focused on one thing: *What we can learn from the results.* Although we are always gratified to learn the positives provided by these surveys—areas in which teachers perceive we are performing well as a school—we are even more anxious to learn of areas falling on the other end of the spectrum—the areas our teachers feel need our immediate attention. Although our specific purposes for surveying may vary from survey to survey, ultimately we survey staff for one general reason: We want to improve our school. To move forward we must know where we currently stand. Therefore, we almost always close any teacher survey with the statement, "Please share with us any ideas you have for improving our school." Some of our greatest improvement initiatives have originated with teacher responses to this statement.

First-year principals have a particular need to get a sense for the *state of the school* according to teacher perceptions. Upon being named principal of any school, we recommend that the new principal set as the top priority: meeting with each individual teacher on the staff for 15 to 20 minutes. Obviously, in schools with 100 or more staff members, this is a time-consuming process, yet nothing the new principal does can provide as much information about the current functioning of the school. We recommend scheduling these individual meetings as soon as possible after being named principal. During these individual conferences, the new principal should listen as much as possible and talk as little as possible. At this stage of the principalship, the goal is for the principal to become more aware of the teachers' perceptions and beliefs rather than the other way around. We recommend that the principal frame these meetings by asking each teacher on staff three simple questions:

1. Where do you see our school in terms of our strengths?

2. In what areas will we need to focus as we move forward?

3. What can you do to help?

Other than posing these three questions, the principal should simply serve as an active listener, taking notes on each response. By meeting with each teacher and asking the same questions, three or four central themes begin to emerge, which provide the new principal with insights regarding the staff's perceptions of the school's strengths and weaknesses as well as a commitment from everyone that they have the capability and willingness to move the school in a positive direction.

Another way for new principals to become more aware of how the school currently functions is by sending a survey to all staff just before the start of the new school year and asking all teachers to return it completed on their first day back. We always make teachers aware that these are anonymous surveys, yet we have found that a significant percentage of teachers voluntarily include their names when responding. They take pride in making us aware of their professional insights. An example of a survey that Jeff Zoul sent to teachers just before the start of his first year as principal was an extremely simple way to become more aware of issues facing the school:

Teachers,

Thank you for taking the time to respond to my queries below and returning to my box during preplanning. I value your feedback and willingness to make me fully aware of all that occurs at our school.

Thanks!
Jeff

- As your new building principal, how can I best support you during this school year?
- Please list our school's most recent successes:
- In what way(s) does our school need to change?
- What is one thing that you are most excited about this year?
- What is most important to the parents of our students?
- What are our students like?
- What curriculum issues need attention at our school?
- What is the key issue we face in the near future? How should it be resolved?
- How are important decisions made at our school? How effective is this process? Should it be changed? If so, how?
- What would you like me to know that I have not asked?

Nearly every teacher returned this survey and provided thoughtful information, which proved valuable in increasing awareness of both our strengths as a school as well as the difficult situations facing us in the future.

Teacher Leaders

Of all possible ways principals can become more *situationally aware*, perhaps the most fruitful is through the work they do in concert with a strong school leadership team. After identifying leadership responsibilities related to student achievement, Marzano and colleagues (2005) propose a five-step plan for putting their findings into action. The first two steps of their plan focus on developing a strong leadership team and distributing responsibilities throughout this team of school leaders. Fullan and Hargreaves (1992) also recognize the need for principals to lead schools with the help of teachers, suggesting that the principal's leadership is enriched by the talent of teacher leaders within the school. We agree and would add that such teachers also enrich the principal's situational awareness.

Nearly all schools have some version of a school leadership team in place, often organized by principals to manage educational change and implement shared decision making. Wallace and Huckman (1999) state that the purpose of such teams is to support the principal in managing the diverse needs of the school and in implementing strategies for school improvement. According to Bell (1992), effective teams enjoy a working relationship defined by a common purpose, understanding, commitment, structure, and operational procedures. At our own schools, we view the leadership team as having seven roles, purposes, or responsibilities:

1. Decision making
2. Advisory
3. Problem solving
4. Training
5. Modeling
6. Communicating
7. Creating/maintaining a positive school culture

We limit our leadership team membership to 15 in number, finding that anything more becomes unwieldy and constrains, rather than fosters, action. Our team members represent all areas of the school, soliciting feedback from and reporting to between 10 and 15 staff members each. We meet every other week for 90 minutes. Upon arriving at the school, we found that the leadership team as it previously existed focused too much energy on operational matters with too little time on teaching and learning issues; so we enacted a *60 to 30* rule, whereby at least 60 minutes of each meeting is dedicated to teaching and learning issues, with no more than 30 minutes dedicated to operational issues. During this 30-minute period, we often address as a team concerns or questions turned in to individual leadership team members by those they represent. We call these *White Card* issues and created a simple form for teachers to complete when they wish to have a matter discussed and acted on

Leadership Team

Contact Form

Teachers should submit this form to their Leadership Team representative when they have an idea, a question, or concern that needs to be addressed with the Leadership Team. All issues will be addressed and a response provided to the faculty member submitting the question or concern. Please fill out all information. Thanks!

Name _____ Date Submitted _____

My idea:

My question:

My concern:

My suggestions/solutions:

Although we separate each leadership team meeting into two chunks of time for two distinct purposes, the goal of becoming more aware of how we are functioning as a school applies to both. It is equally important that principals are aware of both managerial concerns as well as the teaching and learning situations arising as issues within the school.

Fulfilling the responsibility of situational awareness clearly requires that the principal enlist the support of a strong school leadership team, staffed by teacher leaders who have earned the respect and trust of their colleagues. Not all teachers may feel comfortable making the principal aware of certain situations. But all principals and teachers on the leadership team alike must charge these leaders with making them aware of those situations that otherwise might go unnoticed. This awareness allows us to anticipate and prevent many potential problems that would ultimately affect our students.

Core Components

The *points to ponder* offered earlier are but a few tangible ways school principals can become more aware of the innermost workings of the school. In reviewing the preceding list of ideas suggested for fulfilling the leadership responsibility of *situational awareness*, we determined that they fall into one or more of the following five categories, which seem to succinctly encapsulate what we see as the core components of this leadership responsibility:

Cornerstone #4: Awareness
1. Master Public Relations: Aware principals do not underestimate the value of relationships and purposely connect with all school stakeholders in planned and unplanned ways.
2. Lead From Within: Aware principals actively engage in the day-to-day school functioning to gain first-hand knowledge of situations, actions, and inactions.
3. Tune In: Aware principals know that effective improvement requires deep understanding. To accomplish, they sift and filter through daily conversations and events to discern undercurrents and honest school appraisal.

4.   Listen and Learn:
Aware principals value the knowledge and perceptions of others. They inquire often and are able to distance themselves from their own beliefs in an effort to improve the infrastructure and overall performance of their schools.

5.   Plan for Prevention:
Aware principals predict and readily address possible inadequacies, underperformance, and failures to ensure optimal school health and prosperity.

The aware leader plans for and responds to events during the day, which reveals this focus and exhibits a relentless quest to instill this focus in others within the school. The following illustration provides a brief snapshot of ways in which the principal remains intimately aware of all that occurs within the school as she moves throughout her day.

A Glimpse of the Aware Principal

"As we conclude our fall semester and enter into final exams next week with our students," composes Natalie Parker with pride, I want to thank you for teaching students *how to learn*, as well as teaching them what they need to know and be able to do. As I have watched you work this semester, I have seen great evidence of teachers involving students in the process of linking prior knowledge, describing success, setting criteria, giving feedback, and assessing their own learning. You were aware of what your students needed to learn; and as a result, our students are more aware of how they learn—an invaluable understanding that will transcend your class, next semester, throughout college, and beyond. And on behalf of our student body, I thank you for such an enduring gift." Natalie also asks teachers to keep a holistic perspective in view as final evaluations and grades are realized. In addition, on review of recent electronic grade books, Natalie reveals her appreciation for the minimal zeroes and multitude of formative assessments found within. Natalie also reminds the faculty to collect their folders from the counseling office in preparation for today's Advisement session. Lastly, Natalie shares her confidence that test scores will be greater than ever as a result of this past semester's "teaching and learning with passion!"

Before printing her day's calendar, Natalie notes a newly scheduled meeting today with Mr. Frank Howard, father of Matthew Howard, international baccalaureate (IB) student and tops in his junior class. As a result, Natalie reflects on last night's Academic Bowl Banquet, at which both Mr. Howard and Kevin Daily, Academic Bowl sponsor and IB English teacher, spent a great deal of time talking one-on-one. Thereafter, Natalie heads to the commons area where many students congregate before school. Natalie purposely sits next to Rachel Riles, a senior who is at risk of failing two classes, to check if she is prepared for this afternoon's study skills and test prep session with Cornerstone's graduation coach. Praising Rachel's homework efforts, Natalie asks how Rachel is holding up at home, and reminds her of the class ring she looks forward to purchasing when Rachel achieves all of her academic goals. With a smile, Natalie encourages Rachel to "have a successful day," and heads to find Robert Delatorre. With Robert, she asks how his world geography class with Ms. Carpenter is going, and Robert reveals his uncertainty because he and his peers have not received a graded test or assignment to review in more than a month. Listening intently and commenting that she will check into his concerns, Natalie encourages Robert to "have a successful day."

From the far-reaching view of the common's area, Natalie notes the limited number of teachers at their morning duty stations and outside their classroom doors as the first block bell ushers in the day. She individually thanks Lynn Grimes for her consistent presence at morning duty, realizing none of the six faculty members assigned to the commons area is regularly present. Thereafter, Natalie walks to the counseling suite to obtain and personally deliver the Advisement folders of those usually remiss in picking them up and relaying the content within to students.

Pleased with the minimal number of students tardy to first block, Natalie walks to Kevin Daily's room. Upon arrival, Natalie greets Kevin and thanks him for another successful Academic Bowl team performance. Moreover, she thanks him for his valuable input on the Summer Reading Committee despite his clear discomfort regarding the final decision. In response, Kevin reiterates that he is unsure how "is going to squeeze in all the content necessary to the IB English curriculum without having students read three novels over the summer." Furthermore, Kevin adds that those three novels and subsequent evaluations on the first class days are essential to "setting the academic rigor" in his course—revealing his continued disappointment and disconnection to the school's assessment for learning best practice beliefs.

Listening with keen interest, Natalie thanks Kevin for taking student work seriously and asks what teaching and feedback he usually offers for novels inside the school year. After noting an array of teaching and learning opportunities, such using an inquiry-based program for online learning called *Blackboard* to nurture and propel, Natalie suggests offering the same opportunities over the summer. Kevin reminds Natalie of his annual summer mission trip to Mexico, which prevents him from accessing a computer and allows for only a small amount of time for himself. After reflecting on his own words, Kevin thinks of his students in similar situations and pauses without saying much thereafter. Natalie then offers her assistance with the advanced placement (AP)/IB English teachers' search for summer reading assignments that upheld Cornerstone's assessment beliefs; and to assist, encourages Kevin to review their Professional Learning Community text, *Making Classroom Assessment Work* (Davies, 2000). Moreover, she invites Kevin to join her next week to hear Alfie Kohn address the topic of his text *The Homework Myth* (2006). Kevin agrees to take part, and Natalie thanks him for his willingness to learn and refine for the benefit of students.

Thereafter, as Natalie glances into classrooms and walks Cornerstone's hallways, she notices that, once again, Henry Gill is teaching for Lucy Peterson. She writes herself a reminder to arrange a meeting for Henry, Lucy, and herself as soon as possible to rectify this *turn teaching* situation. Natalie even plans to approach Henry after school to discuss his responsibilities as half-time teacher, necessary accountability, and consistency for students, knowing he will relay the same message to his half-time counterpart, Lucy, long before their meeting.

Next, Natalie greets Mr. Frank Howard and escorts him to her office where she listens to his concerns regarding potential changes to summer reading. Natalie assures him that any summer reading decisions made will directly align with school and county instructional and assessment beliefs. In addition, she invites him to this afternoon's Local School Council meeting where the Summer Reading Committee minutes will be discussed and to Cornerstone's next Parent Academy where he can learn more about and offer input regarding Cornerstone's assessment for learning best practices. Lastly, Natalie encourages Mr. Howard to join her and his son's teacher and Academic Bowl sponsor, Mr. Kevin Daily, during next week's Alfie Kohn address on *The Homework Myth*.

Pleased with Mr. Howard's planned attendance, Natalie visits with Cornerstone's registrar and learns of the larger than expected junior class second semester enrollment. As a result, Natalie meets with the assistant principal in charge of scheduling, Jenna Smith, to inquire about opening up additional second semester American literature and U.S. history courses to satisfy the influx of forthcoming juniors, especially because both courses are state requirements. While there, Natalie asks about the test prep classes created for *at-risk* juniors taking state graduation tests in late March.

During first lunch, Natalie decides to sit next to Robert Delatorre and his friends to inquire about advisement. Moreover, Natalie asks a few students how Ms. Sarah Carpenter's world geography class was today, and if they felt prepared for the final exam coming soon. Listening to uncertainty and general discontent, Natalie reminds them to take part in all the study sessions offered at Cornerstone and to take the last few days of reviewing for the final exam seriously; then she leaves to visit teachers during their lunch to solicit their perspectives on the success of advisement.

Next, Natalie heads to meet Sarah Carpenter in her classroom to discuss concerns derived from her assistant principals, personal observations, parental input, and conversations with students. In addition, Natalie brings with her a printout of Sarah's electronic grade book, a copy of Cornerstone's grading/reporting *non-negotiables,* and a pertinent passage from a Robert Marzano book entitled *Transforming Classroom Grading* (2000).

Encouraged by Sarah's willingness to refine her work, Natalie is pleased to learn that Sarah's electronic grade book didn't adequately reflect the many positive grading and assessment practices occurring more often than surmised. As she monitors transitions to fourth block, she is still thinking about a photo she saw on Sarah's desk of Sarah and Ben Byers, Cornerstone's band director, at Mardi Gras.

Thereafter, Natalie reminds her secretary, Carla, that she will be observing Stephanie Walker's student teacher, Jane Alton, for the bulk of fourth block; because there is a good likelihood that Cornerstone will need an additional English teacher next year because of growing enrollment and increased teacher allotments.

After purposeful observation, Natalie makes the afternoon announcements including an added "thank you" to all teachers monitoring transitions and promptly reporting for duty as well as encouraging each Cornerstone teacher and student to "extend your learning, yourself and your heart."

Core Reflections

Consider the ideal *aware* actions of Principal Parker and use the space provided to jot down examples of each core component found within this glimpse. Next, reflect on your own aware leadership actions and include personal notes affirming your strengths and areas of needed growth.

Cornerstone #4: Awareness
1. **Master Public Relations:**
2. **Lead From Within:**
3. **Tune In:**
4. **Listen and Learn:**
5. **Plan for Prevention:**
Personal Notes:

6

There-ness

Cornerstone #5:

The school principal fulfills the responsibility of visibility by having a strong presence throughout the school, making frequent contact with students and teachers. The *visible* principal is interested and engaged in the daily operations of the school, making daily visits to classrooms and regularly attending all school events.

The fifth of nine leadership responsibilities identified by Marzano, Waters, and McNulty (2005), which fall directly under the purview of the school principal and ultimately relate to student achievement, is one the authors call, *visibility*. Unlike some leadership responsibilities, the strong school leader must execute effectively to impact student achievement, *visibility* requires little in the way of explanation. It is not a sophisticated concept with subtle nuances, nor does it require principals to possess a keen intellect. In addition, nearly all educators concur that our very best principals are highly visible in all areas of the school. Given that the concept itself has widespread appeal and is simple to comprehend, one might think that all principals would have a relatively easy time fulfilling this important responsibility. Yet as we all know, this is not the case. Too often, even principals with the best intentions in this regard find themselves overwhelmed by the daily swirl of both scheduled and spontaneous events requiring their immediate attention and drawing them away from the location most central to their work: the classroom. Although all principals face many obstacles standing in the way of remaining highly visible in their schools, the very best ones value the importance of principal visibility and find ways to honor this commitment to teachers, students, and parents.

In analyzing 13 quantitative research studies examining 477 schools related to this school leadership theme, the authors (Marzano, et al., 2005) found an overall correlation of 0.20 between the leadership responsibility of *visibility* and student academic achievement. Knowing this—and understanding intuitively that their presence makes a difference to all stakeholders—principals at strong schools make it a priority to remain highly visible in all areas of the school, making contact and interacting with students and teachers. Although such principals are visible in all areas of the school, they place a particular emphasis on classroom visibility, making frequent and systematic visits to all classrooms within the school. Blase and Kirby (2000) found that teachers may work harder, innovate more, and feel better about their performance when principals regularly visit their classrooms. They associate principal visibility in the classroom with expectations for instruction. While fulfilling the responsibility of *visibility*, the principal also works to execute both aspects of *affirmation*: A strong principal presence in classrooms and throughout the school affirms the behaviors and beliefs of the very best teachers in the school. It also alerts the principal to the underperformance of less effective teachers.

The principal who effectively fulfills the responsibility of *visibility* does so in a variety of ways. Following are just a few ways that principals can fulfill this responsibility as outlined in *School Leadership that Works* (Marzano, et al., 2005). These suggestions are described in some detail and then followed by a brief list of five thoughts summarizing our experiences in this critical area.

Visibility: Points to Ponder

Transition Times

Outside of daily classroom appearances, there are no better opportunities to fulfill the responsibility of visibility than at the very beginning and end of each school day. As mentioned in Chapter 6, we commit ourselves to spending 30 minutes each morning greeting every student who arrives by car or bus. During this time, both the principal and an assistant principal make it a point to interact with as many students as possible. Although it may be only a brief conversation or just a smile and a hearty, "Good morning," these interactions, consistently carried out, let students know that we care about them and how they are doing at our school. As the year progresses and we get to know students better, these daily exchanges become a chance to monitor how certain students are doing in their various classes and to remind them to complete all their work each day. Although our evidence is anecdotal and intangible, the feedback we receive from students and teachers about our habit of greeting every student at our school each morning suggests that this makes a difference. At a minimum, all students quickly come to know who we are and that we take pride in what we do.

We also remain highly visible each afternoon during dismissal. At this time, we place an administrator at the two primary exits as well as in the common areas of the school. Once again, we use this time to interact with our students and remind them of important school matters. In addition, our presence in the halls and at the exits during this hectic transition time also minimizes opportunities for students to misbehave and helps us uphold our faculty value of promoting and insisting on a safe and orderly learning environment. As we see individual students we know are struggling, we may pull them aside for a brief visit to ask how their day went and remind them to complete any homework assignments that night. Oftentimes, we see student athletes or club members exiting to attend an important after-school event. We use this time to wish them well and let them know that we will see them later on. If nothing else, we are simply *there*, wishing our students a good afternoon. As an added bonus, our teachers see us daily in the halls and at the exits during arrival and departure times. This is something they value and respect, making them more likely to follow suit. Again, it may be difficult, if not impossible, to establish a cause-and-effect relationship, but we feel that we are ultimately improving student performance by maintaining a consistent presence during these crucial times of the day.

Another time of the day when we are consistently visible is during our lunch periods. As mentioned earlier, we regularly sit with a different group of teachers each day for at least 20 minutes during lunch to share conversation, if not lunch itself. In addition, we also make it a point to sit with students periodically during lunch. Like many principals, we enjoy the organized student lunches we convene to recognize achievement of some sort or solicit student feedback from key student leaders, but our informal visits with students during their regular lunch period in the cafeteria are equally important and revealing. At least once each week, we sit with a random group of students in the cafeteria and enjoy lunch or just conversation together. We have found that at all three levels of kindergarten through grade 12 (K–12) education, students enjoy having us periodically visit with them during lunch. During these visits, we ask students about their favorite teachers and favorite classes and ask them what they like about our school. We also ask them what they would change about our school if they could. In addition to discussing school-related issues with students, we also enjoy just getting to know them and their interests outside of school. More importantly, we believe that students who come to know us as people who care about them are more likely to meet the expectations we establish for them in terms of learning and behavior.

A final and obvious way we are visible on a regularly scheduled basis at our schools occurs in the hallways during all transitions between classes. At our school we have administrators walking through the halls during each passing period. Even if we are in the middle of something important, we always interrupt what we are doing to monitor the halls between bells. Our presence in the hallways helps students move to their next class in a quick and more orderly fashion. In addition, it sends a powerful message to our teachers that having adults present in the hallways between classes is an important way to prevent potential problems and another opportunity to interact with both teachers and students in an informal way.

Extracurricular Events

Extracurricular activities play an increasingly important role at each level of K–12 education. Strong principals realize the importance of such events and make it a habit to attend as many of these activities as possible. When principals cannot attend, they should make certain that an assistant principal attends. We work hard to plan our school calendar for the entire year and make sure we arrange for administrative attendance at all school events. To make certain we are keeping abreast of changes in the calendar, we meet for 15 minutes each Friday afternoon to review extracurricular school events for the upcoming week and make sure that an administrator is assigned to each. Like most principals of large schools, attending all events has become an increasingly problematic challenge because of the sheer volume of athletic teams and clubs we have in place at our school. At one of our high schools, we have more than 70 clubs and more than 20 interscholastic athletic teams. Obviously, it is impossible for any one person to attend every event scheduled. For major events such as home football games, we require that all administrators attend and remain highly visible throughout the contest. This is a not only an excellent opportunity to interact with our students, teachers, parents, and community members in a different setting, it is also necessary that we monitor such large events to ensure that everything is running smoothly and address any problems that arise. Although all administrators should attend all major events, the school principal should, at a minimum, attend at least one event during the year for every student team and club. At the high school level, this means that at some point during the school year, we attend events for swimming, lacrosse, tennis, golf, baseball, softball, chess club, the equestrian team, cheerleading, debate, wrestling, dance team, drama, chorus, cross-country, student council, Beta Club, and volleyball—to name just a few!

Obviously, attending this many activities requires a huge commitment of time and effort on the part of the principal, yet we feel that going the extra mile by being visible at as many events as possible is well worth the effort. Certainly, many research studies at the high school level (Broh, 2002; Castle, 1986; Eccles & Barber, 1999; McNeal, 1995; and Silliker & Quirk, 1997) have established that a relationship exists between student participation in extracurricular activities at the high school level and performance on school outcomes. At the middle school level, Zoul (2006b) found that middle school students who participated in interscholastic athletics fared better than nonparticipants in terms of grade point average, attendance, and behavior. If we, as principals, know that extracurricular activities can improve student performance, we must commit to supporting such programs through our beliefs and our behaviors. The most important behavior we can exhibit is simply being visible at as many events as possible. Although successful principals may attend extracurricular events partly because research studies suggest it makes a difference in terms of various educational outcomes, they also do so for another reason. They know that each time the principal attends a student activity, at least three people feel better as a result: the student participating in the event, the parent of the student, and the principal himself. Any veteran principal at any level can offer hundreds of examples when their presence has made a difference in their own lives as well as those of students and parents.

Let me share just one recent example. After working a typical week at school, which required my presence on campus for approximately 60 hours, I woke up early to attend two Saturday morning basketball games. To be completely frank, I had no desire to follow through on my final commitment for the week: I had made an off-the-cuff remark to one of our wheel-chair-bound special education students that I would try to attend his basketball game Saturday afternoon. This was not a school-sponsored event and it was taking place an hour or more away from our school. After watching the two morning basketball games, the idea of not attending the wheelchair game and explaining to the boy on Monday that I was simply too busy crept into my thinking. There are more than 1,000 students at our school and my absence at this event would influence just this one student. In addition, I wanted to spend time with my own daughter that day and there were a number of household chores I planned on tackling that afternoon. Although feeling a bit resentful at this encroachment on my time, I made the drive and arrived just in time for the tip-off of the wheelchair basketball game. Before I even saw the student I had come to watch play, my attitude changed. The parents of this boy hurried over when they spotted me. They both hugged me and thanked me for being there. The mother said, "All Marc could talk about last night was that you were coming to his game. We kept telling him that you were too busy and not to get his hopes up because you might not make it." Feeling a bit guilty, but extremely happy that I had followed through on my promise, I settled in to watch an hour-long game that ended in a 0 to 0 tie. In terms of action, honesty compels me to admit it was the most uneventful contest I had ever witnessed. Yet, my simple presence at this game seemed to have a greater affect on this student and his parents than I had ever noticed at the thousands of events I had previously attended. Although my presence seemed to make a small but positive difference in the life of this young man and his parents, it also made a profound difference in someone else's attitude: my own. I was humbly reminded that my presence was important, at least to this one special child, and I was extremely thankful to have made this small extra effort to be there for him.

As principals, we know that extracurricular activities are subordinate in importance to our core business of academic achievement. Yet, we recognize that a relationship exists between the two and that we are responsible for being visible at these events. Successful principals know that most of our parents are much more likely to see us at a football or basketball game than in a classroom. They are even more likely to form judgments about us based on our attendance and actions at such events as opposed to our performance during the school day. Although this is unfortunate and unfair, it remains a reality for many principals. The best ones accept this reality and appreciate the importance of attending as many student events as possible. As a result, they embrace any opportunity they have to be seen supporting students outside the classroom.

Visibility in Classrooms

Principal visibility is extremely important at arrival and dismissal times, in the cafeteria during lunch, in the hallways during transition times, and at extracurricular events. Yet clearly, our primary focus in terms of visibility must be the classroom. At our school, this is the administrative team's non-negotiable job number one. As we begin each new school year, we recommit to our goal of being in every classroom, every day. We cannot accomplish this goal unless we make a plan for achieving it and make this our first priority each day. In our current assignments, we work in schools staffed by a principal and several assistant principals. Each week, we devise a schedule for each administrator to visit various classrooms. At the middle school level, we tend to focus on assigning a specific administrator to a specific grade level each day. At the high school level, we assign an administrator to observe all classrooms within a specific academic department each day. Although we hold each other accountable for adhering to these scheduled visits, we also try to drop in, even if only for a minute or two, other classrooms not on our assigned schedule. In a typical school day, we spend approximately two hours in classrooms and have developed strategies for making sure we visit all classrooms and for making the most of our time while doing so.

Finding the time to visit classrooms is often the bane of existence for even the best-intentioned principal. One way to ensure that we get into classrooms each day is by keeping our mornings clear of appointments if at all possible and, instead, getting out into classrooms as soon as the school day officially begins. Others have devised entire strategies for visiting classrooms and conducting collaborative methods of supervision, such as the Downey Walk-Through (Downey, Steffy, English, Frase, & Poston, 2004). We try to focus on what we call the four Fs in terms of our classroom visibility. We try to make our visits to each classroom Frequent, Fast, Fun, and Fact-finding. Admittedly, this is a bit simplistic; those in search of esoteric theories or highly detailed systems focusing on principal visibility in the classroom may want to look elsewhere. Our overarching goal in this critically important area is simply to *be there* as frequently as humanly possible.

We have already described how we prioritize our time to make certain that each administrator conducts frequent visits to classrooms. One other practice that we have adopted that has resulted in more frequent classroom visits relates to where we do our paperwork. We believe that we are unlikely to affect significant school improvement or influence student achievement while confined to our offices, at least during the hours that students are present. An exception, of course, is hiring new and outstanding teachers. Any time we hire a better teacher to replace a mediocre one, we have improved our school dramatically. But for those few tasks which must be conducted in the office, such as interviewing prospective teachers, we try to schedule them at times when students are not in school. We have found that much of the work that principals typically complete in their offices during the school day can actually be completed in classrooms while teachers and students are working on their own work. Some of the tasks we typically complete in classrooms instead of in our offices include signing time sheets for cafeteria and custodial staff; writing notes to teachers, parents, or students; examining student test data; reading articles related to teaching and learning; compiling student and teacher attendance records; signing various payroll checks; and creating agenda items for upcoming meetings and events. The fact that we have to complete these tasks somewhere is obvious. By completing them in a classroom instead of an office, we get a chance to monitor student learning and teacher performance at the same time that we complete our own work. In addition, our students come to view us as professionals who have their own tasks to complete, and they respect the fact that we do our work at the same time they are doing their own.

Another way we get into classrooms outside our regular visits is by actually teaching whenever appropriate. Typically, teachers enjoy having us teach their class on occasion and students often respond positively to these *guest* teachers. We know of no better way to fulfill our role of *instructional leader* than by actually getting into classrooms and teaching. Our administrative team is currently staffed by leaders who also hold certification in the areas of math, language arts, social studies, and special education. In addition, between us we have more than 80 years of teaching experience. We still enjoy putting this knowledge and experience to use by teaching lessons whenever possible. Often, these are spontaneous moments, when we happen to walk in on a lesson and find that we have insights of our own to share which will reinforce learning. At other times, we may actually arrange in advance to come in and teach an entire lesson on a topic of particular interest to us. In addition to conducting guest lessons in classrooms, at times we visit classrooms to make announcements of importance and that we feel merit a personal visit to students as opposed to an intercom or video announcement. Each year, we visit all classrooms during the first week of school to discuss expectations for student work and student behavior. We have arranged midyear visits to all classes when we have noticed a significant problem occurring in our schools, such as graffiti in the bathrooms. We have visited individual classrooms to announce celebrations, such as a teacher being named teacher of the year, as well as tragedies, including the death of a teacher or student. By visiting classrooms to make announcements, teach lessons, and complete administrative tasks, in addition to our scheduled and unscheduled observations, we ensure that we are in classrooms frequently.

Although we are *frequently* visible in classrooms, many of these visits are also *fast*. There are times, of course, when we all must conduct formal and lengthy observations of teachers. If we spend 2 hours a day in classrooms, we may only get to two classrooms when we are conducting formal observations for the purpose of evaluation. Conversely, when we are simply trying to see our students and teachers at work and have them see us, we can use this same 2-hour chunk of time to visit 24 classrooms for 5 minutes each or 12 classrooms for 10 minutes each. Although we value the importance of brief and extended observations, whenever possible we err on the side of getting into more classrooms for a shorter amount of time as opposed to just a few classrooms for an extended amount of time. Although we make these *drive-by* visits to classrooms every day, on Fridays, if at all possible, we try to visit every classroom in the building for even shorter visits, sometimes lasting less than a minute. On these occasions, we simply like to greet our teachers and students and tell them to have a safe and happy weekend.

While making *frequent* and *fast* classroom visits, we also like to make them *fun*, when appropriate. When entering classrooms, we typically try to do so as unobtrusively as possible. Because we are in classrooms every day, students are practically immune to our presence by now and simply go about the business at hand. Depending on each particular visit, we may involve ourselves in the learning as a way to make our visits to classrooms fun for students, teachers, and ourselves. Typically, we can tell immediately upon entering a classroom if the students and teachers would prefer that we simply observe silently or if there might be an opportunity to join in the fun of learning together. More often than not, we rely on our teachers to invite our participation. As an example, it is extremely common for us to walk in on the middle of a lecture and have the teacher ask our opinion about a specific point. We may also join in a *Jeopardy* review game and answer a question for one of the teams competing for most correct answers. In our physical education classes, we may even join in as students exercise or shoot free throws. We often stress to our students that working hard and having fun go hand in hand and that oftentimes our greatest fun comes as a result of our most difficult work. We try to embody this *work-hard, have-fun* philosophy with our teachers and students in classrooms whenever appropriate.

Our visits to classrooms are *frequent* and often we make *fast* work of this in that our visits can be extremely brief. Whenever possible, we also strive to make these visits a *fun* occurrence for students, teachers, and ourselves. At the same time, however, whenever we visit classrooms we are on a *fact-finding* mission. Regardless of how fast we conduct our visits or how much fun we might have, our primary purpose is to observe and learn more about what is occurring in our classrooms each day. A simple practice we employ to achieve our goal is to sit down next to a student and quietly inquire, "What are you learning today?" At first, this may not elicit much in the way of a response from students; but by consistently asking this question and probing for specific replies, we have learned a great deal about what our students are—and are not—learning each day. Although it happens with much less frequency than in past years at our school, we still walk into classrooms and find students watching a full-length video of some sort. If we sit next to a student and pose our, "What are you learning today?" question, we might receive two distinctly different replies, which help us determine whether this is a waste of valuable instructional time or a legitimate learning activity. A student might answer, "Nothing; we're just watching a movie." Or she might answer, "We are watching this movie to see what slave life was actually like on a plantation and to learn about the Underground Railroad." We have found that even at the elementary school level, student responses to this straightforward question can be quite revealing and provide us the factual information we are seeking.

In addition to soliciting information from students regarding what is being learned, we also learn a great deal from examining what is displayed on the classroom walls and on the boards at the front of the room. Many teachers in our school have the course curriculum standards displayed prominently in their room, along with the day's objective(s) and activities written clearly for all students to see. They also have a word wall with academic vocabulary words strategically placed on one wall of the classroom. Even the tidiness of the classroom suggests something about the learning which is occurring. All the preceding ways of gathering evidence about learning and the learning environment can be accomplished through brief, but regular, classroom visits. In reflecting on our beliefs regarding classroom visits, we like to hearken back to three questions previously posed in this book:

1. What is our purpose?
2. Will this accomplish our purpose?
3. What will our best teachers think?

Our primary purpose for visiting classrooms is to improve both student and teacher performance. When we are consistently in classrooms, we believe we are achieving this goal. As an added benefit, we have found that our very best teachers embrace our daily presence in their classrooms. They take pride in what they do and enjoy having us on hand to witness them sharing their passion for learning with their students.

Core Components

The preceding *points to ponder* are but a few of the tangible ways school principals can become more visible throughout the school and at school events. In reviewing the previous list of suggested ideas for fulfilling the leadership responsibility of *visibility*, we determined that they fall into one or more of the following five categories, which seem to succinctly encapsulate what we see as the core components of this leadership responsibility:

Cornerstone #5: Visibility
1. Prioritize Your Place: Visible principals recognize that wherever they spend the most time communicates what they most value. And they know that the most important and value-worthy school work lies outside of the office.
2. Plan Your Presence: Visible principals ensure their attendance at all formal and informal school activities by purposeful design and dedicated follow through.
3. Commit to Classrooms: Visible principals affirm and reinforce the importance of teaching and learning by actively engaging in the work of teachers and students. They routinely attend daily lessons and become regulars in the classroom.

> **4. Learn First Hand:**
>
> Visible principals acquire direct and intimate knowledge of school instruction, day-to-day operations, relationships, and undercurrents by working alongside all school stakeholders. With such knowledge, they can optimally assess individual and overall school performance.

> **5. Take the Time:**
>
> Visible principals often extend themselves beyond the school day, attending an array of extracurricular events and building personal relationships with students, faculty, parents, and the greater school community. Every school stakeholder is of equal importance and equally worthy of the principal's attention.

The visible leader plans for and responds to events during the day, which reveals this focus on visibility and exhibits a relentless quest to instill this focus in other educators at the school. The following illustration provides a brief snapshot of ways the principal remains highly visible within the school as she moves throughout her day.

Glimpse of the Visible Principal

"Just like our students, I have learned much from you this week," composes Natalie Parker with gratitude. "For example," Natalie relays, "I have learned that you learn how to craft a meaningful descriptive essay by eating apples, you can effectively review for final exams by using cause and effect *people hunts,* you can culminate a semester's worth of learning in one dessert, and Henry Gill can sing about the first 200 years of American history with humor and accuracy." Natalie also notes that she is pleased to learn in this week's department meetings that so many spoke about the importance of being present each day. Moreover, Natalie recalls the large turnout at last night's Advanced Studies Night and anticipates and encourages an even greater crowd for tonight's final football game. She also reminds the faculty that many Cornerstone students have art pieces showing at the local coffee house; and, as she witnessed on Tuesday night, the pieces are selling fast and are wonderful. In particular, senior art student, Rachel Riles, created a piece entitled *Ladybugs* that now hangs proudly in Natalie's daughter's bedroom. Finally, Natalie thanks all teachers who have organized and will be involved in tomorrow's *Saturday Study Session* as she looks forward to teaching right alongside them. Until then, Natalie encourages all to "Teach and learn with passion!"

After printing her day's calendar, Natalie accepts an e-mail invitation to visit Anna Klein's second block physical science class to witness the student's culminating presentations. Confirming her morning schedule with Carla, the school secretary, Natalie heads out to the commons area before the school day officially begins.

While in the commons, Natalie finds Rachel Riles to tell her how much her daughter loves her painting, visits the band room to ask how practice is going, and visits the media center to see if any newcomers are using the early morning extended hours. Very pleased to see Robert Delatorre working diligently on his geometry, Natalie greets Robert warmly and lets him know his efforts have not gone unnoticed. With Robert is Patrick Green, whom Natalie recognizes from lunch the day before. Natalie also greets Patrick and asks if he is preparing for final exams. Before answering, Patrick invites Natalie to watch him play in Saturday night's "Battle of the Bands." After a brief pause to review her past week that was full of extracurricular events every night except Wednesday and with tonight's football game and tomorrow's study session in view, Saturday night was Natalie's only reprieve from school-related events. Yet, with Patrick's evident enthusiasm and genuine desire for her attendance, Natalie willingly accepts his Battle of the Bands invitation and replies that she looks forward to hearing him play.

As she does every Friday after monitoring morning transitions, Natalie joins students in classrooms, conducting first-block walk throughs inside every one. While visiting, Natalie spends moments in some classes saying, "Good morning," or asking if they are preparing for final exams next week, if the lesson seems to allow. In others, Natalie silently observes and quickly moves on. Within some, Natalie takes a few minutes to ask students "What are you learning today?" and intently listens as students provide answers, oftentimes with ease and substance. In one class today, anticipating Natalie's usual Friday class visit, a student hands Natalie a letter from his parents, which she accepts with thanks.

Natalie is pleased to see that Lucy Peterson is present and teaching her assigned first block instead of turn-teaching with Henry Gill. As a result, Natalie makes a concerted effort to tell Lucy, "It is great to see you today! I am so pleased you are here on this important Friday." Natalie shares the same message with those few teachers who are absent too frequently and moves out into the hallways as the transition to second block begins.

During transition, Natalie stops in the nearby girls' bathroom. While there, she jokes with a few putting on make-up and compliments one in particular for her wonderful performance as Snow White in the community's local theater company, which Natalie and her daughter saw last weekend. Both agreed that Cornerstone should look into putting on plays geared for younger children so feeder elementary schools and the greater school community can take part. Remarking that she looks forward to the student's performance in the next Cornerstone play, Natalie moves into the halls to monitor and visit with passing students.

After the tardy bell rings for second block, Natalie stops in the front office to find a parent waiting to see her. Natalie greets the parent and escorts her to her office. Within, Natalie listens to Mrs. Green complain that her son, Patrick, has not been afforded the opportunity to properly review for his final exams, specifically he has not been provided study guides for next week's tests. In addition, Patrick has come home every day complaining that his teachers are unavailable for extra help, and there have been no tutors available in the morning peer tutoring sessions as advertised. As a result, Mrs. Green asks for an extension for all of Patrick's final exams until after winter break. After listening with interest, Natalie reveals that she has personally taken part in the tutoring sessions almost each day and can attest that peer tutors have been present with abundance. Moreover, Natalie shares her communication just this morning with Patrick and knows his focus is clearly on his band, especially his Battle of the Bands event tomorrow night, which Natalie plans to attend. From there, Mrs. Green is open to the recovery suggestions; and Natalie puts Mrs. Green in touch with Kevin Daily, Patrick's international baccalaureate English teacher, to personally arrange one-on-one tutoring time during tomorrow's Saturday Study Session. Pleased with the outcome, Mrs. Green leaves Natalie's office remarking that she looks forward to seeing her tomorrow night; her son can play a "mean bass guitar."

Thereafter, Natalie joins Anna Klein and her physical science students as they present their culminating projects to each other for the reminder of second block. Encouraged by the student performances, Natalie monitors transition to lunch and visits Patrick Green and his friends in the lunchroom. She also makes a concerted effort to speak with Rachel Riles and as many Cornerstone students as possible without encroaching on their time to visit with friends during lunch. Natalie also stops by the teachers' lunchroom to chat about school- and non–school-related topics. She then glides by the counseling suite to check in and wish all counselors a relaxing weekend amid Christmas shopping and next semester's preparations. Next, she visits with the bookkeeper to say, "Hello," and pick up the check needed for tonight's hospitality dinner planned for the football game before walking around the portable classroom, where some students tend to linger and skip lunch if adults are not present.

From there, the bell for fourth block rings, and Natalie chooses to stand in the middle of the commons area to ascertain the most far-reaching view of students in transition. After the tardy bell rings, Natalie moves to the student parking lot to monitor the work-study students leaving campus. In the lot, Natalie sees Robert Delatorre and stops him, knowing he should be in Anna Klein's fourth-block physical science class. Robert shows Natalie his excused-leave note because of a doctor's appointment that couldn't be rescheduled, indicating that his father should be here any minute to pick him up. Robert reassures Natalie that he is prepared for all his final exams, and Natalie escorts Robert to the front office, where he should have been waiting for his father. When Mr. Delatorre arrives, Natalie reminds Robert that only work-study students and seniors should be in the student parking lot at any time and looks forward to his compliance in the future. Robert apologizes and tells Natalie that he looks forward to seeing her at the Battle of the Bands tomorrow night. In fact, Robert mentions that it is "very cool" of Natalie to attend. Natalie then walks Mr. Delatorre out to his car, and while outside, Natalie sees Susan Ericson, English Speaker of Other Languages teacher and department chair, leaving the campus in her car, yet Natalie cannot recall Susan's early leave request. Still reflecting, Natalie waves goodbye to the Delatorres and goes inside to see if Susan spoke with either assistant principal before she left campus.

Next, Natalie makes the afternoon announcements including a note of "thanks" to all teachers present on duty, out monitoring during transitions, and in attendance each day. Natalie also thanks, in advance, students and teachers for their attendance at tonight's last football game and tomorrow's Saturday Study Session. Moreover, Natalie encourages each Cornerstone teacher and student to "extend your learning, yourself, and your heart."

Core Reflections

Consider the ideal *visible* actions of Principal Parker and use the space provided to jot down examples of each core component found within this glimpse. Next, reflect on your own visible leadership actions and include personal notes affirming your strengths and areas of needed growth.

Cornerstone #5: Visibility

1.   *Prioritize Your Place:*

2.   *Plan Your Presence:*

3.   *Commit to Classrooms:*

4.   *Learn First Hand:*

5.   *Take the Time:*

Personal Notes:

7

Cultivating Personalized Professional Relationships

Cornerstone #6:

The school principal fulfills the responsibility of relationships by demonstrating an awareness of and interest in the personal lives of teachers, acknowledging and responding to significant events that occur in their lives throughout the year.

The sixth of nine leadership responsibilities identified by Marzano, Waters, and McNulty (2005), which fall directly under the purview of the school principal and ultimately relate to student achievement, is one the authors call, *relationships*. The authors suggest this responsibility is the "bedrock of the principal's efforts to establish a purposeful community" (p. 103). Oftentimes as principals, we focus on building strong *professional* relationships, emphasizing professional collaboration and valuing *collegiality* over *congeniality*. Yet, we agree with the authors that solid professional relationships cannot be realized without first establishing meaningful *personal* relationships. Our deeper goal as educational leaders may well be to foster a spirit of *collegiality*, which Little (1981) defines as the presence of four behaviors in the school setting: (1) talking about practice, (2) observing each other, (3) working on curriculum; and (4) teaching each other. We suggest that it is impossible to achieve such an atmosphere in any organization without first valuing, cultivating, and maintaining a spirit of *congeniality*, adults working together who enjoy each other's company and care about what is happening in each other's lives. The principal must make congeniality an important foundation on which to build a community of collegial learning.

In analyzing 11 quantitative research studies examining 724 schools related to this school leadership theme, Marzano and coauthors (2005) found an overall correlation of 0.18 between the leadership responsibility of *relation-*

ships and student academic achievement. *Knowing* that fulfilling this responsibility ultimately leads to improved student achievement, strong school leaders set about *doing* specific things associated with building personal relationships, a leadership trait not emphasized in previous models of leadership. Goleman, Boyatzis, and McKee (2002) suggest that in the old model of leadership, the focus was one of functionality, with people in the organization viewed as interchangeable parts. Increasingly, in today's organizations, this impersonal type of leadership fails and the most effective leaders lead not through positional power, but by excelling in the art of relationships. By caring about those people with whom they work, effective leaders build fierce loyalty and inspire people in the organization to give their very best.

Extraordinary accomplishments within our schools cannot be achieved without the principal and teachers working together. They become personally involved with both the work and each other to succeed. Although the principal must initiate this focus on personal relationships within the school, ideally this attitude of caring becomes a mutual and synergistic force in which all faculty and staff are responsible to each other. Such an outcome is aptly described by Kouzes and Pozner:

> Social interaction and support work both ways—as you give, you get, and you become interconnected and caught up in people's lives. It always takes a group of people working together with a common purpose in an atmosphere of trust and collaboration to get extraordinary things done. (1987, p. 270)

The principal who effectively fulfills the responsibility of *relationships* does so in a variety of ways. Following are just a few ways that principals can fulfill this responsibility as outlined in *School Leadership that Works* (Marzano, et al., 2005). These suggestions are described in some detail and then followed by a brief list of five thoughts summarizing our experiences in this critical area.

Relationships: Points to Ponder

In reviewing the Points to Ponder sections in Chapters 2 through 6 of this book, it becomes evident that the responsibility of *relationships* pervades each of the other responsibilities principals must effectively execute to serve as purposeful leaders whose actions ultimately affect student achievement. In each of the preceding five chapters, we have offered several specific suggestions for fulfilling one of the other leadership responsibilities. Many of these practical ideas in each of the five preceding chapters are also appropriate ways of fulfilling the leadership responsibility of *relationships*. In Chapter 2, which examines the responsibility of *optimizer*, we include our practice of sending holiday greeting cards to family members of all teachers. Although this practice is an ideal way to optimize the performance of those with whom we work, it is even more directly an example of how we show an interest in the personal lives of our colleagues. In Chapter 3, in looking at the responsibility of *affirmation*, we share many ideas that principals can use to affirm teacher performance. Yet, many of these affirming practices are also relationship-building practices. Our Teacher Hall of Fame is but one example. As we induct teachers each year into our Hall of Fame, we also invite their family members to our brief ceremony to add even more to the personal, as well as professional, significance of the accomplishment.

Chapter 4 highlights the leadership responsibility of *ideals/beliefs*. In this chapter we share examples of the many ways we engage our students and staff in community service projects. Although these activities teach our kids important lessons and help those in need, they also fulfill another purpose: By working side by side with teachers in our school on community service projects, we are building the personal relationships, which will also strengthen our professional resolve. In Chapter 5 we provide ideas for serving as a *situationally aware* principal. Many of these ideas are also associated with relationship building, such as simply sitting down with a group of teachers each day to enjoy a quick lunch and some pleasant conversation. Although we often discuss school-related issues during these informal lunches, we more often end up talking about our families and our outside-of-school interests. Finally, in Chapter 6 we stress the importance of serving as a highly visible principal. As we suggested in this chapter, an important time for principals to be visible is during transition times between classes. This is also an ideal time to build relationships with teachers. As we walk the corridors each day during these transitions, we are able to greet our teachers in the hall who are also monitoring students and quietly thank them for being there or inquire about a personal matter, asking about an ill family member or congratulating them on the performance of their son or daughter at last night's game or band concert.

Building Positive Relationships with Teachers

Building positive relationships with teachers is the foundation for all that we do as principals. To effectively fulfill any leadership responsibility, we must first demonstrate an awareness of our teachers' needs, interests, and special circumstances. We must show them that we care about them as individual human beings, not just as employees. As educators, we are all in the *people* business. Principals model this focus on people by demonstrating an interest in the personal lives of the teachers within the school.

Many of the ways we work to establish positive relationships with teachers have been described in previous chapters because they also fulfill other leadership responsibilities. However, there are several additional practices worth mentioning here that specifically address our focus on building relationships. An important personal, as well as professional, accomplishment for any educator is gaining some level of new education. We tend to make a big deal about any educational advancement our faculty and staff have achieved. At the close of each semester, we ask our teachers to let us know about any accomplishments they have made in furthering their own education. The most frequent recognitions we make in this area include honoring teachers who have completed an advanced degree. Nearly every semester, we have at least one teacher or administrator who has received a master's, specialist's, or doctoral degree. We also recognize our paraprofessional workers who go back to school to obtain their bachelor's degree or complete additional coursework and pass tests to become highly certified paraprofessional educators. In addition, we often have teachers who enroll in a series of courses to obtain certification endorsements such as ESOL, gifted, or reading. We even have custodians and cafeteria workers who take courses to update their knowledge in important areas related to their field of expertise, facilities and school nutrition. Another accomplishment we always recognize publicly, which is both a personal and professional achievement, is publishing an article of some sort or presenting at a conference. The preceding examples of personal and professional growth are important opportunities for celebration. We always recognize these at our faculty meetings, in our newsletters, and in personal notes to teachers.

We make it a point to recognize important personal events in the lives of our teachers including birthdays; weddings; births; and, unfortunately, deaths and illnesses that occur each year. Every Monday morning, we send out an e-mail communication to the staff that includes the week's events. Within this e-mail, we always include the name of any staff member who is celebrating a birthday that week. We also give a birthday card and a free ice cream pass to teachers on their birthdays. Staff members who get married or welcome a new baby into their family are also celebrated. Typically, we have an after-school party to honor these important personal events and our school's Sunshine committee uses donations to its fund to purchase gifts from the school. Although we make every effort to notice and actively participate in these and other staff celebrations, we are even more focused on being there for teachers experiencing the loss of a family member or any other personal tragedy. Although nothing we do can erase the pain our teachers feel during these times, we make every effort to attend funeral services; visit staff members who are in the hospital; send notes of sympathy or concern; and provide meals, money, or any other support we can offer. In such situations, each teacher has unique needs and methods of coping; and we strive to honor this, treating each situation differently, depending on the desires of the family. In the past 3 years, we have established scholarship funds, purchased a wheelchair, organized a fun run/walk, and delivered weekly meals to staff members who were in need of support.

The Power of Language

A small, yet significant, area on which we focus to help build positive relationships is our spoken and written language. Specifically, we use several simple words as often as possible when working with our teachers: *please, thanks, we,* and *our*. As with most things we do in working with teachers, this is also something we want our teachers to do with the students they teach. Saying *please* and *thank you* requires absolutely no effort and spoken consistently and sincerely over time is almost certain to pay regular dividends. We never ask a teacher, custodian, secretary, or any other staff member at our school to do anything without saying *please* and *thank you*. Whether this is a face-to-face communication or a written communication, we are vigilant about including these words to accompany any request we make or direction we give. As I began my career as a principal, a trusted veteran principal friend advised me to delegate every task that could possibly be delegated because there are simply so many tasks which can *only* be completed by the principal. To the extent that this advice is sound, that means that most principals are assigning a huge number of tasks to be completed to other members of the staff. Adding simple words of courtesy and respect when asking others to complete a task makes people feel valued. Say "Please," a lot. Say "Thank you," a lot. People with whom you interact will notice this and appreciate it.

Two other words that take on monumental importance in terms of relationship building at our schools are the pronouns *we* and *our*. We cringe when we hear principals say, "At *my* school," or "*My* counselor thinks." To thrive as a strong school marked by sustained success, all stakeholders must possess a feeling of ownership about every event that impacts the school. We realize that principals innocently use phrases similar to the preceding; but consistently replacing the word *my* with the word *our* is a subtle, yet effective, way of communicating that we are all equal *owners* of our schools. Substituting *we* for *I* whenever possible is also an effective way of sending a subtle message that the *school needs* to exist in a certain way rather than communicating that the *principal wants* the school to exist in a certain way. Examples abound in our daily lives as school leaders. Stating to faculty members, "We need to examine how we performed in the area of math computation last year," trumps "I noticed that our math computation scores were subpar last year." When posting job vacancies, school systems almost always list *effective oral and written communication skills* as a core requirement necessary for success, yet we often overlook the power of our daily language as we interact with those already serving at our school. We suggest that words such as *please, thank you, we,* and *our* are relationship-building words. Those who work with us come to notice this over time and after matching our actions with our words, realize that these words align with our actual practices.

The End of the School Year

Celebrations are a huge factor in building strong personal relationships with teachers. We have already outlined many ways we celebrate student, teacher, and school performance. At other times, we celebrate merely to enjoy each other's company. We may convene holiday gatherings as a staff or family movie nights on a large screen in our auditorium, or a family bowling night. We established a tradition at one school that became a fun way to celebrate the end of each school year. On the final teacher planning day at the end of each year, we invited every staff member to an outdoor picnic at a nearby park and arranged for a business partner to cater dinner. Prior to this farewell gathering, we visited the local dollar store and bought gifts for each of our 100 staff members. At the end of the evening, the principal would dedicate about 1 hour introducing each staff member, thanking them for their work during the year, and then presenting them with a gag gift, always finding a way to relate a story of some sort which managed to tie in to whatever dollar gift was being given. Amazingly, we were always able to find 100 gifts that we could somehow relate to each of our teachers and only spend $100.00 in the process. Although the presentations almost always included a good bit of humor, we were careful to never cross a line and share an unflattering, off-color, or sarcastic story about the person in our attempt to be funny. Each year, nearly all teachers attended this event and looked forward to the time when these end-of-the-year *awards* were presented.

Personal and Professional

Another way that principals cultivate strong *personal* relationships is by inviting teachers to accompany them to *professional* conferences. About a month ago, a principal from a neighboring system invited Laura Link to attend a half-day conference in our area presented by well-known educational writer, speaker, and thinker Alfie Kohn. The first thing Laura did upon receiving this invitation was request permission to bring along a small team of teachers from her high school who were recently examining their homework practices and discussing Kohn's ideas in *The Homework Myth*

(2006) as they reflected on their purpose and their practice in the area of this ongoing and controversial educational debate. Although Laura's team should gain much from this event professionally, they should also grow in their personal relationships. We have found no better way to build strong personal relationships with our teachers than inviting them to learn alongside us at conferences of this sort. Obviously, money is always a consideration, because professional development funds are never as plentiful as we would like; yet each time we attend professional conferences with our teachers, we notice that we *almost always* learn something about our profession and we *always* learn a great deal about each other.

The Teacher Evaluation Process

We believe that teachers should work at a school because they enjoy the work (students, curriculum, instruction, etc.) and the people they work with (other teachers). In education, financial incentives remain almost nonexistent and most of our teachers enter the profession because of a sincere desire to make a difference in the lives of others. Serving in perhaps the only profession in which financial remuneration is not dependent on job performance makes the issue of performance appraisal a challenge for school administrators. We do not have the power to increase the pay of our superstar teachers nor limit the salary of our mediocre teachers. Yet, performance reviews and evaluations of teachers are required in all school districts and both teachers and principals often struggle to find an effective way of assessing teacher performance. The teacher evaluation process in place at many schools is a potential threat to principal–teacher relationships, because poor teachers are not held accountable for their performance and outstanding teachers are not affirmed for their good work through the appraisal process. Between us, we have worked at 15 schools during our combined 40 years of public school service and are still searching for the perfect teacher appraisal tool. We have come to the conclusion that none exists; if it did, every school in the nation would be using it, of course.

Although no perfect tool or system for evaluating teachers exists, we have refined our own thoughts on this challenging issue over the years. The one thing we decided early in our administrative careers is that this process is important in terms of the relationships we build with our teachers. Anything that we require of our teachers must be meaningful; our teachers cannot view it as a joke or something they must simply check off their *to do* list. We also realize that we cannot manage the performance of our teachers; instead, we must observe their performance and note the results of their performance. We can work together with our teachers to set specific goals related to their performance and provide them the tools necessary to accomplish these goals.

In our summative review of each teacher's individual performance, we hold fast to one key idea: Honest conversation is superordinate in importance to documentation. Too often over the years, we have observed inferior teachers who could produce sterling portfolios of evidence that would lead one to believe they were John Dewey reincarnated. Although we firmly believe that collecting evidence of student learning is important and should play a role in our appraisals of teachers, we grew weary of hearing teachers juxtapose the words *dog and pony show* with the teacher appraisal process in place. We observed teachers at some schools toting wagons full of student work and teacher documentation to a 30-minute end-of-the-year evaluation conference with administrators. Something about the entire process did not seem genuine; we were confusing paperwork and documentation with conversation and feedback. Instead of assessing our teachers' performance in a personal way, it seemed that we were trying to assess their performance by examining their paperwork and filling out more of our own.

Although we have yet to perfect the teacher evaluation process and strongly suspect we never will, at our schools we have made one major paradigm shift in this area. In evaluating teachers, we focus on our relationships with them to improve their performance. Schools are relationship-focused organizations. We cannot build relationships with portfolios, reports, and paperwork; instead, we must build relationships with our people if we intend to maximize their performance and enhance the relationships they, in turn, build with our students. We believe that building relationships with teachers through the teacher appraisal process starts with principals fulfilling two related leadership responsibilities previously discussed in this book: situational awareness and visibility. We have all heard legitimate tales of principals who have never set foot in a teacher's classroom evaluating these teachers on a piece of paper at the end of the school year. Although an extreme example, such practices of evaluating teachers are common within some schools. To form valid assessments of our teachers' performance and provide useful feedback, teacher *evaluation* must begin on the first day of school and must be an ongoing process, culminating in an honest year-end conversation about what went well and what did not. Two weeks before these conversations, we typically provide teachers with five questions on which to reflect that will serve as a basis for discussion during our conference. Three of these questions vary from year to year and may vary from teacher to teacher. Our final two questions tend to remain consistent from year to year. First, we always ask teachers how the work they accomplished in their own classroom added to the overall school improvement goals. Although each teacher is focused primarily on their subject/grade level-specific SMART goals, they must also realize that they are vital in helping the school meet its overarching school-wide goals.

Therefore, if one of our school goals is increased math achievement in the domain of computation, we expect our art teacher to offer ways she worked to reinforce computation skills. Secondly, we always ask our teachers at the end of any evaluative conference how we, as administrators, can do a better job of supporting the work they do in the classroom. We always emphasize improvement in all areas of our school, including administration, and we typically ask teachers how we can improve the school in the future. We also ask each teacher to share ways we already improved the school during the current year. This typically proves to be an affirming and relationship-building process, because together our staff may brainstorm up to 50 or more ways our school improved from one year to the next.

We have high expectations for all teachers and we state our expectations clearly at the beginning of each year and throughout the year. We emphasize that these are not merely administrative expectations for teachers, but our *school's* expectations for teachers which are aligned with our mission, vision, values, and goals. By emphasizing honest conversations and regular classroom visits while placing less emphasis on portfolios and paperwork, we attempt to use the teacher performance review process as an opportunity to build personal and professional relationships among our staff.

Core Components

In reviewing the preceding list of ideas that suggest ways the school principal fulfills the leadership responsibility of relationships, we determined that they fall into one or more of the following five categories, which seem to succinctly encapsulate what we see as the core components of this leadership responsibility:

Cornerstone #6: Relationship Building
1. Extend Yourself: Relationship-building principals offer care, support, guidance, and genuine interest daily to all school stakeholders.
2. Get Together: Relationship-building principals recognize and model that they share ownership of the school by speaking and acting inclusively and fostering mutual respect.

> **3.** **_Honor Honesty:_**
> Relationship-building principals engage in critical and meaningful conversations with all school stakeholders, especially those who may be underperforming. By directly addressing areas of necessary growth, uncertainty is quieted and positive performance is collaboratively affirmed and sought.

> **4.** **_Work Alongside:_**
> Relationship-building principals do not merely delegate school work; they actively take part in formal and informal school duties and responsibilities. They also share personal and community-focused experiences inside and beyond the school day.

> **5.** **_Readily Recognize:_**
> Relationship-building principals regularly acknowledge noteworthy personal and professional events through systematic and informal means. They value all by honoring them as family members, learners, and colleagues.

The relationship-building leader plans for and responds to events during the day, which reveals this focus on relationships and exhibits a relentless quest to instill this focus in other educators at the school. The following illustration provides a brief snapshot of ways in which the principal remains highly focused on positive, professional relationships within the school as she moves throughout her day.

A Glimpse of the Relationship-Building Principal

Natalie Parker entitles today's e-mail correspondence, "Thank God, It's Monday" as she welcomes faculty and staff returning from the weekend. She writes, "Because 'life is a great bundle of little things,' as Oliver Wendell Holmes once observed, it is important that we take advantage of every single experience we share with our students and each other. And to best accomplish this goal, let us treat every person *right in front of us, right now, in the right way.* To start, I would like to thank all teachers who took time out of their weekend to tutor during Saturday's Study Session. We had record-breaking student and teacher attendance, and many students were able to receive one-on-one instruction and care. In addition, Friday's final football game of the season was also very well attended; the stands were packed with familiar faces and Cougar spirit and pride was pervasive. Thank you for sharing your time and your families with us; it was great to visit and cheer with all of you.

In addition, Natalie shares that colleague Lynn Grimes just received her acceptance into next summer's Educational Leadership Specialist cohort and that Jill Stevens got engaged (finally!) to the fabulous beau everyone knows and approves of. Natalie invites everyone to extend "congratulations" to both.

She also reminds everyone of their holiday party this Thursday evening, encourages attendance during today's third-block Lunch and Learn, and looks forward to speaking with the department chairs during today's second-block Articulation meetings. She concludes with an invitation to "Teach and learn with passion!"

After printing the day's calendar, Natalie checks her mail and greets an array of teachers with a welcoming smile. She asks each, as a minimum, "How was your weekend?" With most, Natalie asks specific questions. For example, she asks Kate Johnson how her students fared on the advanced-placement essays she graded over the weekend; Susan Ericson if her daughter is feeling better after last week's tonsillitis surgery; and Aaron Bell if his student, Robert Delatorre, was progressing after a week of morning tutoring in geometry. In addition, Natalie offers a "Thank you," and "Have a great day" to each as she walks out to the commons area in search of newly engaged Jill Stevens on duty.

After personally congratulating Jill, Natalie waves, smiles, and briefly chats with passing teachers and students until the start of first block. Thereafter, Natalie heads to visit classrooms, yet she is flagged down by Lynn Grimes before entering one. Natalie redirects her path to greet Lynn and asks how she can assist. Lynn thanks Natalie for the acknowledgment in today's morning e-mail and asks Natalie if she would be willing to be her official mentor for her Educational Leadership cohort. Natalie readily replies and expresses that she would be honored to serve as Lynn's mentor and assist in any way. Moreover, Natalie offers her personal books and resources for Lynn's use at any time, invites Lynn to sit in on future Leadership meetings, and promises to include her in county-level leadership opportunities necessary to fulfill practicum requirements of her degree program. Lynn gratefully thanks Natalie and shares that she plans to take her up on all offers.

As Natalie steps into Aaron Bell's geometry classroom nearby, she can tell that he is not himself, because he never sits in a chair while teaching. And even though Aaron says he will be OK, Natalie persists until he reveals that he may have the flu. As a result, Natalie strongly encourages him to seek medical help or go home and rest while she fills in for the remainder of this class and collaborates with peers to assist with class coverage throughout today. Moreover, Natalie says she will make an announcement canceling his Habitat for Humanity meeting after school today and hopes that he feels better soon.

After finding departmental substitute coverage for the rarely absent Aaron Bell, Natalie places free lunch coupons in the mailboxes of the teachers subbing for Mr. Bell today before monitoring the transition to second-block.

While in the hallway, Natalie approaches as many teachers as possible. She calls them by their first names, inquires about their day, and simply thanks them for being present before making her way to the counseling suite and today's scheduled Articulation meetings.

Natalie, along with every counselor and Assistant Principal Jenna Smith, scheduled time with each department chair starting today to reflect on the semester's departmental successes and areas of needed growth. They also review present course offerings, course alignments, and teacher allocation in preparation for next year's change to the seven-period day from their current block schedule. Science chair Pam Stone is first to take part as she is welcomed with a firm handshake and smile by Natalie. Listening as Pam shares thoughts and concerns generated by her department, Natalie asks Pam to elaborate. Pam willingly reveals that there is great anxiety among her science teachers as to how to conduct successful and meaningful labs inside 50-minute classes. As it is, with 90 minutes, they are hard-pressed to complete labs from start to finish. Taking notes, Natalie recalls a recent visit to a neighboring county high school where they added 50-minute lab classes adjoining selected science courses, and she invites the group to discuss such a possibility. Pleased with the potentiality of lab classes, Pam notes that she is always so appreciative of the counseling team's understanding and willingness to work with her and the department for the good of students at all times. Natalie agrees with Pam and adds that she looks forward to their follow-up Articulation meeting in February before student registration begins. Lastly, Pam says she learned that Aaron Bell went home sick and offers to facilitate his Habitat for Humanity meeting today because a guest speaker from Home Depot is coming. Natalie thanks Pam with sincere gratitude.

After meeting with Pam, Natalie and the Articulation Team collaborate and learn with two other department chairs before third-block lunch begins. And after speaking with the lunchroom staff regarding today's new addition to the menu, Natalie purposely heads to Stephanie Walker's classroom before the Lunch and Learn begins.

Meeting Stephanie at her desk, Natalie reveals that an adoption agency called her for a reference on Friday afternoon. Natalie was hopeful that perhaps some progress was underway and inquires what the next steps in the process are. Learning that the call was routine, Natalie extends a comforting hug reassuring Stephanie that she will be a mommy soon enough.

Next, Natalie and Stephanie join the Lunch and Learn facilitated by the county's Director of Educational Leadership Dr. Paige Dupree. Today's learning topic is on Relational Leadership, a necessary skill, according to Natalie, at the heart of building trust and integrity within any community; and she is so excited that Dr. Dupree has agreed to share and learn with them. Both Natalie and Dr. Dupree are active participants in the local Rotary Club and have facilitated community round-table discussions on the same topic to great success. In fact, through her service in the Rotary, Natalie has generated four new Partners in Education for her school and two for the school district. Together, Natalie and Stephanie join Dr. Dupree and 32 teachers electing to take part in today's learning session. As usual, Natalie is heartened by the large volunteer turnout and makes sure she communicates her appreciation for the obvious value each participant places on their own professional learning.

Energized by the positive and reflective conversation during the Lunch and Learn, Natalie escorts Dr. Dupree to her car, visits a few fourth-block classrooms, and returns to her office for the first time since the morning. While there, she listens to a voicemail left by Stephanie Walker's husband, Scott. Within, he thanks Natalie for taking the time to complete the numerous character references, maintaining confidentiality, and fielding phone calls from adoption agencies on behalf of him and Stephanie. More importantly, he thanks Natalie for supporting his wife throughout and always assuring her that she can rely on and trust in Natalie without fail. In conclusion, Scott extends his deep gratitude and comments that he "looks forward to thanking her in person during Thursday's holiday party."

Smiling, Natalie reflects on the generous phone message and all that she has listened to and learned today. Next, her afternoon announcements include a reminder about this afternoon's Habitat for Humanity meeting in Pam Stone's room and a passionate encouragement to each Cornerstone teacher and student to "extend your learning, yourself, and your heart."

Core Reflections

Consider the ideal *relationship-building* actions of Principal Parker and use the space provided to jot down examples of each core component found within this glimpse. Next, reflect on your own relational leadership actions and include personal notes affirming your strengths and areas of needed growth.

Cornerstone #6: Relationship Building

1. Extend Yourself:

2. Get Together:

3. Honor Honesty:

4. Work Alongside:

5. Readily Recognize:

Personal Notes:

8

Clear and Consistent Communication

Cornerstone #7:
The school principal fulfills the responsibility of communication by establishing and maintaining strong lines of communication with and between teachers and all stakeholders.

The seventh of nine leadership responsibilities identified by Marzano, Waters, and McNulty (2005), which fall directly under the purview of the school principal and ultimately relate to student achievement, is one the authors call, *communication*. It is a responsibility the authors suggest is a feature of most aspects of leadership. Effective communication is not a new concept; we have all heard that communication is a key to success in any organization. All businesses and schools seek to hire outstanding communicators, those who can clearly express both verbally and in writing a wide variety of issues important to the entire organization. Communication is clearly one of the most powerful tools available to leaders in moving an organization forward, yet it remains a challenge for many and teachers regularly cite *lack of communication* as a downfall of the school or school leader.

The importance of effective communication is so profound that principals simply cannot succeed as school leaders without excelling in this leadership skill. Evidence suggests that as much as 70% of school administrators' time is spent in the area of communication (Kmetz & Willower, 1982). Other studies have found that student achievement increased in schools with climates characterized as more open (Mikkelsen & Joyner, 1982). In recent years we have witnessed a proliferation of communication tools, yet sheer quantity of communication methods is not the route to effective communication. Our efforts at communicating effectively must focus on quality not quantity, and we must focus on the outcomes we are looking for through our communications as opposed to the communication device or message itself. We communicate to our teachers, students, and other stakeholders for a wide variety of purposes. We must examine our practices to determine whether they are aligned with our intended outcomes. As with most leadership responsibilities, we need not necessarily focus on *more* communication; rather, we must focus on *purposeful* communication.

Strong school leaders know that communication is a two-way process; both sender and receiver must play active roles. Principals must ensure that they participate in both roles, working not only to send important messages to staff but also taking time to actively listen to those within the school. Communication in the school setting is also used for a variety of purposes, from sharing the daily schedule of events to reiterating the mission and vision of the entire school. In this chapter we focus more on the former rather than the latter. We feel that communicating the *big picture* topics relating to our school are closely related to establishing and maintaining an overall school culture, which we examine in Chapter 9.

In analyzing 11 quantitative research studies examining 299 schools related to this school leadership theme, Marzano and coauthors (2005) found an overall correlation of 0.23 between the leadership responsibility of *communication* and student academic achievement. *Knowing* this, strong school principals set about *doing* things to ensure effective two-way communication with and among all stakeholders, especially the teachers with whom they serve. The principal who effectively fulfills the responsibility of *communication* does so in a variety of ways. Following are just a few ways that principals can fulfill this responsibility as outlined in *School Leadership that Works* (Marzano, et al., 2005). These suggestions are described in some detail and then followed by a brief list of five thoughts summarizing our experiences in this critical area.

Communication: Points to Ponder

Thank God It's Monday!

All principals strive to consistently communicate the school's mission, vision, and values. Yet, it is equally important that principals communicate the daily events in the life of a school in a clear and consistent way as well. Perhaps nothing upsets teachers and disrupts learning more than unannounced deviations to the regular schedule. Because we ask that teachers plan for quality bell-to-bell teaching each and every day, we work hard to honor the instructional time and not interrupt this sacred time unless there is an absolute emergency or a worthwhile activity which is planned for well in advance of the event itself. One way we communicate the weekly schedule to teachers is by sending out a weekly e-mail memo each Monday morning, which we call, "Thank God, It's Monday." Although its primary purpose is to spell out every event occurring throughout the week, we also use this weekly memo to communicate a few key messages about teaching and learning, announce staff birthdays, congratulate and recognize students and staff for accomplishments, and offer a faculty trivia question. The title of the memo itself is used to lightheartedly communicate one of our core beliefs: We enjoy the work we do and are happy to be here.

Thank God, It's Monday!

Teachers:

HEY! Our Value: We Will not give up on students and will welcome all students regardless of ability or background .

I received a phone call Friday from the principal at a middle school in Upson County (Thomaston, GA). Her question: how did Otwell MS raise their math CRCT scores so dramatically? The answer, of course, is simply because the entire faculty targeted a need area and committed to improving. Our superior math instructors led the way, but this question is a testament to all who were here last year working on math achievement with all students.

Thanks! Thank you to Andrea Thomas and Paula Flatman for working with our Academic Team this year. Attending this competition each year is one of my favorite events to follow. Our kids always perform well in this competition. Thanks to Jenna, Amy P., and Wendy for attending a Thursday, Friday, and Saturday PLC Conference. I wanted to send a few teachers new to our school to hear the DuFours and Eaker talk about PLCs; I look forward to hearing what they learned. Thanks for supporting the concept of holding our kids accountable for completing all work assigned by supporting our Saturday Academy intervention. A big thanks to all teachers who agreed to cover a Saturday session as needed. Remember that Saturday Academy will meet this Saturday. Thanks to Leah and Pam for volunteering in the concession stand during our home football games; you two are amazing!

Play . . . make their day . . . be there . . . choose your attitude . . . Have an awesome week; teach with passion!

This Week's Stuff:

Monday:

**********	Counseling Dept Fundraiser
**********	Yearbook Gift Basket Raffle Tix on sale
7:45–9:00	Drama Practice
7:45–8:30	BBALL Intramurals 6th grade (gym)
4:15–6:00	Cooking Club (room 513)
4:30–6:30	Football Practice
5:00–6:30	LSC Meeting (conference room)

Tuesday:

**********	Counseling Dept Fundraiser
**********	Yearbook Gift Basket Raffle Tix on sale
7:30–8:30	PLC Small Groups
9:00–9:25	RED BLACK SESSION #1
2:50	Tornado Drill
4:15–9:15	Chamber of Commerce mtg (café)
5:00	FOOTBALL GAME @ LMS!!!!

Wednesday:

**********	Counseling Dept Fundraiser
**********	Yearbook Gift Basket Raffle Tix on sale
**********	Early Release Professional Development
7:45–9:00	Drama Practice
7:45–8:45	BBALL Intramurals 7th Grade
7:45–8:45	Tech Club (Z's Room)
8:00–12:00	Math Adoption Meeting (BOE)
8:00–8:45	Academic Team Meeting (room 236)
2:00	SIOP/Prof Dev (café)

Thursday:

**********	Counseling Dept Fundraiser
**********	Yearbook Gift Basket Raffle Tix on sale
7:45–9:00	Drama Practice
8:00–8:50	Advanced Chorus (room 512)
3:30–4:00	Snack Shack 7-M/S

Friday:

**********	Counseling Dept Fundraiser
**********	Yearbook Gift Basket Raffle Tix on sale
7:45–8:30	BBALL Intramural 8th Grade
8:00–8:45	Academic Team Mtg (room 236)
4:30–6:30	Football practice

Saturday:

9:00–11:30	Saturday Academy

Happy Birthday!!!
Upcoming Birthdays: Mr. McCollum, September 18th!!!

The Essential 55:
Rules for Discovering the Successful Student in Every Child by Ron Clark (2003):

Rule 14: Answer all written questions with a complete sentence. For example, if the question asks, "What is the capital of Russia?" you should respond by writing, "The capital of Russia is Moscow." Also, in conversations with others, it is important to use complete sentences out of respect for the person's question. For example,

if a person asks, "How are you?" instead of just responding by saying, "Fine," you should say, "I'm doing fine, thank you. How about yourself?" (Too often when working with adolescents, we let them off the hook, both in writing and conversationally, by allowing them to simply respond yes or no or in a simple word or two. We help our students when we instill the habit of writing and speaking in complete sentences. This is an excellent way to integrate writing and communication skills into any content area. This helps students develop and organize their thoughts and build a command of the English language).

Faculty Trivia Question (Free Prize for First Correct Answer)

Which staff member plays fullback on a coed soccer team every weekend?

a. Tony Jones

b. Mark Fisher

c. Kathy Ciavarelli

d. Sandi Troxell

e. Carol Swegman

Despite the "Monday" reference in the title of our weekly memo, we typically send this out via e-mail over the weekend, because many teachers are in the habit of checking e-mail on the weekends and planning for the approaching week. The *Thank God, It's Monday* memo is a simple and fun communication tool we use to accomplish several purposes. Although its foremost intent is to communicate every activity occurring in the school during the course of the week, it also is a way to build relationships, affirm staff and student performance, and even communicate a few ideas regarding our profession. This year, we have included a short excerpt from Ron Clark's popular book, *The Essential 55* (2003) each week for teachers to consider in their own classrooms.

The Friday Focus

Although we use the *Thank God, It's Monday* memo to kick off the week, primarily as a way to communicate the week's events, we also send out a weekly communication via e-mail to the entire staff every Friday, which focuses on a specific issue relating to teaching and learning. The idea of a Friday Focus was first used by Whitaker, Whitaker, and Lumpa (2000) as a way to communicate various messages to staff. At our schools, we have used these weekly memos to communicate our thoughts on very specific topics applicable to any teacher in our building. We have written Friday Focus memos on classroom management, homework, questioning, assessment, working with special education students, school safety, bullying, and professional learning to name just a few. Most of these are written by the principal or assistant principal, but we also regularly call on teacher leaders to craft Friday Focus writings. A complete collection of 37 Friday Focus memos written over the course of a school year is included in *Improving Your School One Week at a Time: Building the Foundation for Professional Teaching and Learning* (Zoul, 2006). An example of our Friday Focus communication tool follows, this one dealing with effective questioning techniques.

Friday Focus!

"The most basic way teachers have to stimulate interactive thinking and learning in the classroom is through the use of questions" (Rice & Taylor, 1985).

As a classroom teacher, I often reminded myself that my lessons should be effective, efficient, and relevant. By incorporating focused questioning techniques, teachers can help to ensure effectiveness, efficiency, and relevancy. At OMS, I have enjoyed observing various questioning strategies employed by our adroit teaching staff. Too often, questioning becomes an overlooked component of the lesson.

Obviously, through questioning, we check for individual and whole group understanding. Questioning individual students is most effective; questioning the whole group is most efficient. At times, it is appropriate to opt for efficiency. When so doing, you might consider using signal responses (teaching students to "show" the answer by a predetermined signal). Questioning individual students is more common and therefore requires greater teacher attention. In questioning, all students should believe they are as likely to be called on as any other student. In questioning individual students, I find it more effective to utilize an "ask-pause-call" method as opposed to a "call-ask-wait" technique. In the first case, the teacher phrases a question, giving all students time to formulate a potential response. Then, she calls on a random student to provide an answer. Example: "I'm going to ask you a question and I want everyone to think of an answer. From what you read in our text, what were some causes of the Civil War?"

When calling on an individual for a response, allow ample wait time. Research suggests we should wait 3–5 seconds after asking the question before calling on any individual student. We should allow at least 5 seconds for a response and another 3–5 seconds after obtaining a response prior to reacting. If, after waiting, the student initially does not provide an answer, you might inveigle a response by offering a clue and restating the question. If, after this, the student still had no answer, I would often reply, "That's OK, Suzanne, but pay attention, because I'm coming back to you." Then, I might call on another student to provide the correct answer. Once I received the correct answer, I would return to the original student, getting her to now verbalize the correct answer.

On the other hand, by employing a "call-ask-wait" technique (e.g., "Suzanne, what is a noun?"), the resulting effect is that the anxiety level is raised for one student while everyone else is off the hook and not accountable for responding or even attending. As a teacher, I often found myself reluctant to call on those struggling students who I feared would not be able to respond correctly. By employing an ask-pause-call method of questioning, allowing ample wait time, providing additional clues, and—ultimately—coming back to that student for the correct answer, I felt that I was able to engage all learners more effectively.

I am pleased, therefore, to note that teachers at OMS are skilled in questioning techniques and avoid capricious patterns of checking for individual and whole group understanding. Josef Albers stated with perspicacity, "Good teaching is more a giving of right questions than a giving of right answers." Thanks for taking the time to reflect on your daily questioning techniques. *More importantly, thanks for Teaching With Passion each day!*

Have a great weekend— Jeff

Teachers at our school have enjoyed reading these Friday Focus memos over the years and have also enjoyed taking turns writing about their own areas of expertise or passion and communicating these with their colleagues. Time is always a problem for teachers and administrators in that we never seem to find the time to gather and discuss our daily practices. The Friday Focus is one way we have been able to regularly communicate, in writing, about topics important to our craft.

Professional Learning Communities

Although the Friday Focus serves as a written format for establishing dialogue with and among teachers regarding teaching and learning practices at our school, we also emphasize regularly scheduled face-to-face conversations about learning. Like so many other leadership responsibilities, all principals know that having conversations with teachers about learning is important; the best principals make sure that this becomes a priority and find a way of building time into already-frenzied school calendars for professional dialogue. At our schools, we provide this time in a variety of ways, most consistently through our weekly Professional Learning Community (PLC) meetings. Teachers at our schools dedicate 1 hour each week before the official teacher start of the school day to meet within their PLCs to discuss what we want kids to know, how to measure their learning, how to respond when students do not learn, and how to help each other help our students learn. In addition, we meet every other month as a whole faculty and meet once a month during common planning times for 90 minutes to discuss professional learning. Periodically, we also host *Lunch and Learn* meetings with small groups of teachers to focus on issues we face in our classrooms that become issues of concern throughout the school year.

Faculty Book Studies

Obviously, all teachers attend every regularly scheduled whole- and small-group faculty meetings, and we work hard to keep the focus at all such meetings on student and teacher learning. An additional and optional learning forum we host each school year is our administrative book studies. Each administrator at our school chooses one professional book each year to read and invites teachers to join them in examining the selected book. This year our four administrators chose the following four books to read and discuss: *There are No Shortcuts* by Rafe Esquith (2003), *What Great Teachers Do Differently* by Todd Whitaker (2004), *The Learning Leader* by Doug Reeves (2006), and *The Courage to Teach* by Parker Palmer (1998). Each of us invites teachers to gather twice a month during our first semester, usually in the morning, to share their thoughts on what they have read and to determine if anything they have learned is something we might try in our school or share with other colleagues not participating in the book study. As a school, we typically purchase books for any teacher willing to participate, and we provide a simple breakfast each time we meet. Each book study group generally contains only a small number of teachers, but this time together always proves to be an enjoyable forum for examining our current practices in light of the professional reading we are examining. Our administrator book studies are strictly voluntary and most teachers do not always participate, but these small group learning sessions provide a unique way to dialogue about education and build relationships with teachers in a more informal and intimate setting.

Effective Listening

Listening is an oft-overlooked key to effective communication. Principals, it seems, are especially susceptible to focusing much more on what they are saying than what they are hearing. This is a natural tendency, because we are charged with leading the school and leading any organization clearly requires that the leader communicate regularly to stakeholders both in writing and in conversation messages related to the core business within. Moreover, principals lead hectic existences, with increasing demands on their time, seemingly every day. It requires a conscientious effort, therefore, to focus on active listening when working with our teachers. For our students to learn as much as possible, there are many times in the classroom setting when we want them to actively listen to teachers. The same holds true in working with teachers. By practicing these same active listening habits as teachers, we model a desired behavior for students. Principals who actively listen to teachers also send a powerful message. We show them that we care about them as individuals. In addition, we may well gain new insight into another person's perspective about a difficult issue facing our school or an individual at our school.

In stressing *active* listening, we emphasize the following aspects:

- ◆ Make eye contact
- ◆ Give your undivided attention
- ◆ Send nonverbal signals that you are interested and that you care
- ◆ Be able to paraphrase what is being stated when appropriate
- ◆ Don't interrupt (McEwan, 2003)

By adhering to all the preceding practices, we try to guard against sending the message that we do not have time to listen—no matter how desperately we may feel that to be the case because of our busy schedule! When a teacher needs to speak with us, we commit to honoring this person by truly listening to them. If the situation arises spontaneously and we simply cannot take the time to immediately devote our attention to a teacher's needs, we respectfully ask if we can talk with them about the issue later that day and suggest a few times that might work better. We are firm believers that as leaders and learners we accomplish more from asking questions and listening than we do by answering questions and speaking.

Meetings with Meaning

As mentioned earlier, we hold our fair share of meetings at our schools, from whole faculty meetings, to planning period meetings, to PLC meetings, to leadership team meetings. Although these meetings all take up valuable time, they are important and teachers have come to view them as important. Each of the preceding meetings has a different purpose. Although whole faculty meetings at our school are times for celebrating success and sharing strategies, our PLC meetings are for working collaboratively to examine specific curriculum issues. To earn teacher commitment to the importance of each meeting, we adhere to one basic rule: Everything on every meeting agenda must be important. This sounds silly, but it came about after one of the very first leadership team meetings Jeff convened shortly after being named principal. He found himself saying something along the lines of, "If you will look at your agenda, you will note that we have several important items to discuss." Realizing the stupidity of this statement, he caught himself nearly in midsentence and added, "I suppose if we eliminate the unimportant items, we can all get out of here a bit early." In laughing, then thinking, about this, our leadership team came to the realization that teachers honestly felt that they spent a lot of times at meetings discussing or receiving information about topics that were neither urgent, nor important. We immediately vowed that no meeting time would ever be used to disseminate insignificant information or information that could not otherwise be communicated through an e-mail or some other, more efficient method. In addition, we pledged to never discuss a topic or address an issue with the entire staff which only pertained to an individual or a group of teachers. Finally, we always find a way, however small, to incorporate fun into our meetings.

We often use the term *Meetings with Meaning* when considering whether to hold a meeting and developing agendas for meetings. If there is no legitimate *meaning* to why we are gathering, we do not *meet*. Again, this sounds painfully obvious, yet we have sat in on hundreds of meetings in hundreds of schools where the meaning of the meeting was either unclear or unimportant. At our schools we do hold many meetings, with many different purposes, but we never meet merely for the sake of meeting. The primary shift in our perspective regarding the meetings that we schedule at our schools was in moving from meetings that focused on management/operational issues to meetings that focused on teaching and learning issues. Put another way, we use meetings to communicate ideas about our school culture.

In addition to these meetings we schedule at our school to address teaching and learning, professional development, and school culture issues, periodically, we find the need to call the entire faculty together for 5 minutes or less to make a very brief, but important announcement. This may occur four or five times during the course of the year. At our school we have a large, circular area in the center of the school that we call the *rotunda*. Whenever we need to hold an impromptu meeting, we simply call teachers to meet for a 5-minute Rotunda Roundup. Within 1 minute, the entire staff can assemble in the rotunda. We use this very brief meeting format to announce something we feel must be shared in person, such as the death of a teacher or student; the announcement of a staff member's new baby or wedding; the news that our school has received a special award; or the news that one of our staff members has earned a special honor or recognition, such as being named our state Teacher of the Year.

At our schools, we meet regularly and fairly often in a variety of different formats and groupings of staff. Although few educators suggest that they actually enjoy meetings, we have found that by conducting focused meetings with a specific purpose, sticking to the stated agenda, meeting only when necessary, limiting agenda topics to items that cannot be communicated more efficiently, and incorporating fun into meetings, our teachers more readily accept that the work conducted in our meetings is important to our school.

Communicating Good News and Bad News

We tend to follow the general guideline that we never deliver bad news in writing. If we have a teacher who is underperforming or makes a mistake of any sort, we insist on meeting with that individual in person to discuss the area of concern. It is not always the most comfortable or easy way of dealing with personnel issues, but we feel it is the most honest and effective way of confronting our teachers who fall short of expectations in any area. Conversely, we communicate good news to groups of teachers and individual teachers in a variety of ways. Each administrator at our school follows a simple practice to communicate positive comments to our teachers: writing one note card every school day of the year—which, for us, is 180 days. We have four administrators at our school, so between us, we write 720 note cards to teachers during the course of the year. We have 110 teachers on staff, which includes custodians, cafeteria workers, and office personnel; so a strong probability exists that each staff member will receive one or more cards from an administrator throughout the year.

Although this may seem like an ambitious undertaking, carried out consistently, it requires no more than 10 minutes each day. We purchase inexpensive blank note cards at dollar stores and anywhere else we can find them at the beginning of the year and distribute these to all administrators. Although we each have our different methods for writing our daily notes, the focus is the same: to communicate, in writing, any type of positive news we know about one of our teachers. At times, these words may be a follow-up to an effective lesson we observed during an informal classroom visit. We might also write to thank a teacher for sponsoring an extracurricular activity or congratulate a coach for an important victory. We may write to a teacher thanking them for mentoring a first-year teacher or going the extra mile for a student in need. The content can vary, but we try to be brief and genuinely praise a very specific behavior or accomplishment. Some of us write one card each morning upon arriving at school. Others write them at home or during a visit to a teacher's classroom. Afterward, we simply place them in teachers' mailboxes. Our teachers seem to appreciate the fact that we take time to recognize them in this simple way. In addition, we have found that each time we praise one of our teachers in this manner, someone else ends up feeling uplifted, too: the administrator who wrote the words on the card.

Core Components

In reviewing the preceding list of ideas suggesting ways the school principal fulfills the leadership responsibility of *communication*, we determined that they fall into one or more of the following five categories, which seem to succinctly encapsulate what we see as the core components of this leadership responsibility:

Cornerstone #7: Communication
1. Value Connections: Communicative principals recognize the importance of regular and meaningful exchanges through verbal and written means.
2. Open Channels: Communicative principals ensure and foster two-way, fluid correspondence through active inquiry and listening.
3. Model the Message: Communicative principals articulate and write with clarity and intelligence. They appreciate language and respect its power.
4. Design Dialogue: Communicative principals build the structures and capacity necessary for purposeful and ongoing professional conversation inside and beyond the school day. They compel the participation of all school stakeholders.
5. Show and Share: Communicative principals reveal their values and beliefs through their considered actions. They are attentive and responsive in posture and presence.

The communicative leader plans for and responds to events during the day, which reveals this focus on communication and exhibits a relentless quest to instill this focus in other educators at the school. The following illustration provides a brief snapshot of ways the principal remains highly focused on communicating clearly, consistently, and effectively within the school as she moves throughout her day.

A Glimpse of the Communicative Principal

"Thank you for demystifying what students should know and be able to do," writes Natalie proudly. "Because you clearly communicated student learning goals this semester through regular and consistent use of preassessments, standards, rubrics, study guides, self-assessments, benchmarks, conferencing, and more, our students are well aware of final exam expectations and how to best prepare. In addition, by involving parents in student-led conferences, you have ensured an audience for student work that is an informed and integral part of the improvement process. And when Ralph Waldo Emerson said, 'The man who can make hard things easy is the educator,' I am convinced he was speaking of you."

Natalie continues with a reminder about final exam particulars, which are posted on the Cornerstone web site as well as in each teacher's classroom. First and third blocks will test tomorrow and second and fourth blocks will test the day after. Natalie asks each teacher to review the attached modified final exam bell schedule, post in classrooms, and announce the lunch schedule noted within.

Natalie also notes that today's PLC's during planning blocks will provide each Content Collaboration Team time to refine and review feedback plans for final exams. As an option, Kyle West, Cornerstone's Instructional Technology Specialist, is offering tutorial sessions covering Blackboard, an online discussion medium for students and teachers that can even be used over the holiday break.

Also in late February, Natalie asks advanced placement (AP) and international baccalaureate teachers to mark their calendars and plan to attend Advanced Studies Night on the 26th from 5:00 to 8:30 p.m. Natalie reveals preparations for the event will occur during a January PLC, and that she will send an Outlook calendar invitation so each can place this event on his or her electronic calendar. She adds that it is already on Cornerstone's web-based master calendar, and on this last day before final exams, Natalie once more invites every teacher to "Teach and learn with passion!"

Before printing today's calendar, Natalie reads a few e-mails that require her immediate attention and response. For example, she replies to Jill Stevens' requests regarding the school newspaper and confirms an unexpected meeting request sent by Kate Johnson, AP coordinator, set for first block today. Lastly, Natalie writes to Harvey Nichols, head custodian, asking that he check the girls' bathroom in the 1200 hall. As Natalie was walking the building this morning, she found that a few sink faucets were leaking. Natalie thanks Harvey, in advance, for his help.

Next, Natalie meets Jenna Smith and Andrew Sutton, assistant principals, before school starts. Natalie addresses the school newspaper, which is first on the agenda. She relays that Jill Stevens is anxious to print this edition before she leaves for winter break so students can have the newspaper at the start of next semester. All concur that the timeline is sound, yet all agree that the article "Drugs and Teens" is not acceptable in its current state, because it doesn't offer positive solutions to the problems it poses. They agree that the *Teacher's Corner* is a wonderfully informative addition, and Natalie takes responsibility in relaying their decisions to Jill Stevens.

Secondly, they divide communication responsibilities for Advanced Studies Night to ensure a successful event. Jenna will make sure the event is posted on the school's front marquee a week prior, send out an auto-dialer phone message, and advertise it on the school's web site. Andrew will post the event on every school bulletin board, provide an event flyer to each teacher for classroom posting, and assist Natalie with the mass mailing of the principal's invitation letter. Third, Natalie emphasizes the importance of student support plan communication to all classroom teachers before students served through such plans enter classrooms. Both Jenna and Andrew agree that front-end communication should quell accommodation inconsistencies revealed in their fall parent survey. As a result, they divide up the responsibility of ensuring hardcopies of 504s, Student Support Team (SST) plans, and Individual Educational Plans (IEP) to all stakeholders on the first day back from winter break. And after discerning athletic event coverage during the winter break and finalizing plans for Thursday's holiday party, Natalie thanks Jenna and Andrew before she exits.

Natalie joins Jill Stevens on duty in the commons area to relay the decisions made about the upcoming edition of the school newspaper. Natalie reminds Jill that she will officially articulate their concerns in writing so she can share them with her journalism students for editing and refinement.

Thanking Jill for her efforts and understanding, Natalie retrieves a call from Carla on her walkie-talkie. Carla asks if she would be willing to seek out counselor Joanna Price because Kathy Dalton, counseling secretary, shared that a very concerned parent was with her. Confirming, Natalie heads toward the counseling suite and enters Joanna's office threshold asking if she can assist.

Upon entering Joanna's office, Natalie greets Ms. Sharon Sams by name, extends a firm handshake, makes eye contact, and sits upright in the chair beside her. Both Joanna and Natalie listen to Ms. Sams express her serious concerns regarding geometry teacher, Mr. Bell, and that she has heard that most of his students are failing his course and not receiving the extra help when asked. Natalie supports Joanna's encouragement to speak directly to Mr. Bell first, because it is Cornerstone's communication protocol to do so. Moreover, Natalie requests that when she does indeed speak with Mr. Bell, she address the specific concerns regarding her daughter without hearsay, because her faculty are not at liberty to discuss other student grades and performance or wholesale class averages. In addition, Joanna shares the communication log that Mr. Bell forwarded to her 4 weeks ago concerning her daughter and reiterates that every teacher is required to contact parents every 4 weeks at a minimum if a student is failing a course to provide tutorial and recovery options. Thanking them for their time, Ms. Sams exits with plans to contact Mr. Bell right away. Natalie offers her appreciation and walks Ms. Sams to the door with a handshake and warm, "Thank you."

Asking Joanna Price to keep her updated regarding Ms. Sams, Natalie walks to Kate Johnson's classroom for their AP Intent meeting. While there, Natalie sits besides Kate as they diligently review the AP Intent form. Both worked on clarifying the message that asks students to mark all AP exams they intend to sit for in May and indicates that by signing the form, they clearly understand the financial obligation that comes with ordering, not taking, the exams. Natalie asks Kate to include contact information for both of them just in case students and/or parents have questions. Thanking Kate, Natalie leaves to take part in first block's PLC.

Pleased with the focused conversation in all PLC groups, Natalie monitors transitions between classes, and joins the second-block Articulation meeting with all counselors and English chair, David Rodriguez. Leaning forward, Natalie listens intently to David, without interruption, relay his thoughts regarding the affect of a 7-period day on assigning and grading essays. When David is clearly finished talking, Natalie compliments his insights and forethought, repeats some of his concerns, and agrees that they must offer support to all teachers regarding balancing of assessment load, especially essay assessments. Counselor Joanna Price adds that she is aware of an online essay submission program that can assist with teacher feedback and alleviate some of the formative grading load. As a result, David thanks Natalie and the counselors for their time and care.

Thereafter, Natalie heads to second block's PLC session and then to Kathy Dalton's desk to pick up the proofread copy of her January Principal's Letter. With minimal changes suggested, Natalie plans to get the letter to the copy center and mailed off to all Cornerstone students and their parents right away.

Next, Natalie heads to the lunchroom to again seek out senior Rachel Riles, check in with the teachers on lunchroom duty, assist with trash pick up between lunches, inquire about the new cash registers, and take a moment to read a few of the scrolling television announcements highlighting today's tutoring sessions. Natalie then joins third block's PLC session.

Natalie calls Carla on her walk-talkie after the final bell for fourth block rings, letting her know she will be observing in a few classrooms before participating in fourth block's PLC and returning to make the afternoon announcements where Natalie invites every teacher and student to "extend your learning, yourself, and your heart."

Core Reflections

Consider the ideal *communicative* actions of Principal Parker and use the space provided to jot down examples of each core component found within this glimpse. Next, reflect on your own communicative leadership actions and include personal notes affirming your strengths and areas of needed growth.

Cornerstone #7: Communication

1. Value Connections:

2. Open Channels:

3. Model the Message:

4. Design Dialogue:

5. Show and Share:

Personal Notes:

9

Creating
a Culture

Cornerstone #8:

The school principal fulfills the responsibility of culture by fostering a combination of values, beliefs, and feelings among teachers, which promotes a sense of community and cooperation, accompanied by the creation and use of a common language regarding teaching, learning, and schooling.

The eighth of nine leadership responsibilities identified by Marzano, Waters, and McNulty (2005), which fall directly under the purview of the school principal and ultimately relate to student achievement, is one the authors call *culture*. In reviewing nearly any book or article related to the topic of *school culture,* one is almost certain to see it referred to as *the way we do things around here.* One is also likely to note the words *school culture* juxtaposed with *change.* Changing a school's culture is often necessary to improve teacher performance and student learning. However, it is also important to define what we, as principals, will *not* change: the values, traditions, and relationships that must be preserved even in the face of change (Reeves, 2007). In changing the school culture, Reeves knows that effective leaders build on prevailing norms rather than suggesting that everything currently in place is ineffective and irrelevant. School culture is of paramount importance to both the new and veteran principal; and changing the existing culture, according to Barth (2001), is the most difficult job of an instructional leader.

The power of a school's culture is that it carries with it the ability to influence everything about the group, from discussions that occur, to beliefs widely shared among teachers, to the core values embraced, and—most importantly—to the expectations we hold for our students and each other (Goldring, 2002). A school's culture can dictate what is and is not discussed in public and in private. Barth (2001) contends that each school has a list of what he terms *nondiscussables,* from "the leadership of the principal" to "race" to "the underperforming teacher." Schools with positive cultures have few, if any, nondiscussables. To eliminate—or at least limit—nondiscussable issues within the school setting, principals must work purposefully to establish a healthy school culture. Saphier and King (1985) identified 12 healthy cultural norms:

1. Collegiality
2. Experimentation
3. High expectations
4. Trust and confidence
5. Tangible support
6. Reaching out to the knowledge bases
7. Appreciation and recognition
8. Caring celebration and humor
9. Involvement in decision making
10. Protection of what's important
11. Traditions
12. Honest and open communication

Goldring (2002) has identified a list half as long, but with much in common, identifying six key traits of culture:

1. Shared vision
2. Traditions
3. Collaboration
4. Shared decision making
5. Innovation
6. Communication.

In reviewing both lists of traits associated with creating a positive school culture, it is easy to see how these qualities can dramatically affect a school's capacity to improve in a variety of ways, most importantly in terms of student and teacher learning. It is also obvious that both studies have identified similar traits characteristic of productive school cultures (experimentation vs. innovation and involvement in decision making vs. shared decision making). Finally, it is clear that many of the traits essential to establishing or changing a school's culture are also directly related to nearly every leadership responsibility discussed in this book from *affirmation* to *relationships*, to *situational awareness*, to the final leadership responsibility discussed in Chapter 10, *input*. A school's culture constitutes what occurs in the school as well as the manner in which events occur; and the principal must cultivate and maintain a culture that promotes, rather than inhibits, the cultural traits stated preceding.

Most often, the issue of school culture presents itself to principals as they begin their tenure at a school and identify cultural norms in need of changing. In building lasting cultural change, Reeves (2007) advises principals to follow four essential practices. First, principals must identify parts of the school culture that will *not* be changed. Even in schools with counterproductive prevailing cultures, good can be found; and principals must not send the message that every current practice is bad and must be changed. Second, principals must focus on actions. Too often, school principals say all the right things as they assume the principalship, but our teachers are more interested in our actions. Our very best teachers are hoping we will follow through on our vows to instill collaboration, innovation, shared decision making, and celebration as part of the way we do business. Talking about doing this is not enough; we must act in a manner that shows we are serious. Third, we must use the right change tools for our school or district, based on variables such as the extent to which teachers agree on what they want and how to arrive there. Finally, principals must be willing to engage in what Reeves calls the "scut work." As we have suggested previously and will no doubt do again, the small things we do as principals mean a lot—to our teachers, our students, and our parents. In terms of cultivating a positive school culture, teachers notice, respect, and respond to the principal who takes over a class periodically, picks up trash in the lunchroom while monitoring student behavior, or works with a student one-on-one after school as a mentor or tutor. Through these and other small actions, principals convey that all jobs have value and that we are all teaching through modeling.

In analyzing 15 quantitative research studies examining 819 schools related to this school leadership theme, the authors (Marzano, et al., 2005) found an overall correlation of 0.25 between the leadership responsibility of *culture* and student academic achievement. *Knowing* that school culture may relate to student achievement, the strong school principal sets about *doing* those things that promote a positive and productive culture. The principal who effectively fulfills the responsibility of *culture* does so in a variety of ways. Following are just a few ways that principals can fulfill this responsibility as outlined in *School Leadership that Works* (Marzano, et al., 2005). These suggestions are described in some detail and then followed by a brief list of five thoughts summarizing our experiences in this critical area.

Culture: Points to Ponder

Teacher Isolation

Teacher isolation is a phenomenon all too common in schools today, particularly at the high school level where teachers typically focus almost exclusively on what occurs within their own classroom setting, paying little heed to overall school or departmental teaching practices. In recent years many school leaders have attempted to foster a school culture of collaboration where teachers teach each other, sharing strategies and skills related to all aspects of instruction. However, most of this sharing tends to take place in meetings and through informal discussions. At our school we implemented a process whereby this sharing of professional practices occurs in a more relevant manner, with teachers observing each other in action periodically throughout the school year. We ask that every teacher at our school select a colleague to observe teaching a lesson at least once each month. Teachers conduct these informal peer observations during their own planning periods and are free to visit any classroom they choose to learn more about the teaching and learning that occurs throughout the school. We try to keep our expectations for this process clear and simple, asking only that each teacher spend at least 15 minutes observing a colleague each month and fill out a form describing what they saw and learned. The form we use for these observations is simple, too, consisting primarily of two sections, a description of what was observed, along with any commendations or questions that the observing teacher notes (see a sample of our current form following). At one school, we call these observations, *O.M.S. Reports* which stands for both our school name and the words, *Observing Masterful Staff*. We implemented a similar program at the high school level, calling it *O-CATS*, a reference to our school's team nickname as well as an acronym for *Observing Colleagues Actively Teaching Students*.

Our purpose in asking teachers to make it a regular practice of observing each other in action is to promote a culture of true collaboration and professional learning within the most immediate and practical setting—our school's classrooms. By requiring that teachers complete a certain amount of peer observations each year, we are also putting actions behind our words of expectations. Merely communicating with our teachers the idea that it is important that we learn from each other is not enough. Instead, we must expect teachers to do so and design a simple, yet systematic, way of making sure it happens. Not every teacher at our school immediately embraced the idea of spending a few minutes each month during a planning period observing their colleagues, but over time this has become a valued practice that is embedded in our school's culture. In addition to learning new strategies and providing each other with written feedback, these observations tend to be fun, as veteran teachers get to know a first-year teacher and teachers new to our school get to see first hand what everyone has been raving about in another colleague's classroom. After conducting an observation, teachers place one copy of the form in the principal's box and one copy in the box of the teacher they observed. Periodically, we review these reports and send out to the entire staff a compilation of notes that teachers have written about each other. These almost always prove to be affirming and uplifting messages extolling the virtues of many teachers at our school and the best practices they implement on a daily basis. We have found this to be an effective way of breaking down the walls of isolation that still exist in many schools and promoting a culture of sharing, professional learning, and celebration.

Otwell Middle School

Observing Masterful Staff

Reporting Form

Observing Teacher: _____

Name of Teacher Being Observed: _____

Date: _____ Time: _____

Grade Level/Subject: _____

Description of Teaching and Learning Activities:

_____

_____

_____

_____

_____

_____

_____

_____

_____

_____

Wows! and Wonders: _____

_____

_____

_____

_____

_____

_____

_____

_____

_____

_____

_____

Faculty Meetings

Another way we promote a school culture that values the sharing and exchanging of professional practices occurs during our faculty meetings as we regularly reserve the bulk of whole faculty meeting time for teaching one another. Over the years we have implemented this in various ways. During my first year as principal, we simply assigned a different department to *host* a faculty meeting, which consisted of creating a theme of some sort, providing light refreshments, and preparing a 20-minute presentation focusing on some issue relating to teaching that members of that department wanted to share with the rest of the staff. Our school's leadership team hosted the very first meeting and decided to share strategies for improving student behavior in the classroom, because this was identified as a primary concern of teachers during individual teacher conferences. We employed a baseball theme for our presentation, which included printing creative tickets *admitting* each staff member into the meeting (and used for a raffle drawing); wearing our favorite baseball cap; and serving hot dogs, peanuts, and soft drinks. More importantly, we presented nine ideas for improving classroom instruction, adapting the nine-inning format of a baseball game. Each member of the leadership team took charge of one *inning,* which simply meant that they shared a strategy they had incorporated in their classroom to help them manage the learning environment. We even took a seventh-inning stretch, standing and stretching for 60 seconds, and discussed how even something as simple as a stretch can be effective in the classroom to keep students engaged and alert. As the school year continued, each department seemed to enjoy sharing strategies which members considered a specific strength and interest of their teaching area. Our ESOL teachers presented a lesson on cognates in a clever way; our physical education department organized teachers into stations and showed how they rotate students through various learning activities. Our language arts teachers shared a format for incorporating writing into any content area. Our counseling staff shared their expert insights into bullying behaviors, including how to identify signs of bullying as well as how to deal with bullies and victims of bullying. Each presentation over the course of the year proved to be a fun way to exchange ideas which were also relevant to our profession.

In recent years we have held fewer whole faculty meetings in favor of more group-alike professional learning community meetings. However, we still feel that it is important to gather as a whole faculty on a regular basis. Each time we do, we have one major goal for our faculty meetings, which we borrowed from Todd Whitaker (2003) several years ago: to make our teachers more excited about teaching when they leave the faculty meeting than they were upon arriving. The two primary activities we plan to achieve this goal are celebrations and professional sharing. Teachers always enjoy the celebratory activities previously described, which affirm the performance of students, teachers, or the school as a whole. In addition, teachers value our practice of insisting that we teach each other something about our craft every time we meet. We have found that our teachers enjoy both roles; that is, standing in front of the faculty and sharing what works for them as well as listening to a colleague and learning another technique they can try in their own classroom.

By dedicating the bulk of time at each faculty meeting to informal, collegial professional learning, we have helped foster a school culture that values the concept of teachers working together to improve our school. Very early in my teaching career, Jeff also coached basketball for several years and enjoyed attending coaching clinics where successful coaches would simply stand at an overhead and begin drawing out the offensive plays, defensive schemes, inbounds plays, and practice drills that they found to be effective practices with their own teams. We always wondered why faculty meetings were not like this; it made sense that the best way to learn new ideas as a basketball coach was to sit and listen to others share what worked for them. Teaching should be no different. Every teacher at our school knows something about teaching that no other teacher knows. Our goal as administrators is to cultivate a school culture that encourages each teacher to share what they know—their unique passions, strategies, lessons—with every other teacher on the staff. Learning from each other has proven a powerful way to promote a collaborative culture and reflect on our professional practices.

A Common Language

Another way we promote our school culture is by building and communicating a common language for both students and teachers regarding our core business of learning. For teachers, this common language includes, of course, our statements of mission, vision, and values. In addition, it includes language we use throughout the school to describe the work we do in all classrooms. For us, this consists primarily of the 12 "Working on the Work" (WOW) Standards designed by Phil Schlechty (2002), which comprise the WOW framework: Patterns of Engagement, Student Achievement, Content and Substance, Organization of Knowledge, Product Focus, Clear and Compelling Product Standards, A Safe Environment, Affirmation of Performance, Affiliation, Novelty and Variety, Choice, and Authenticity. See Schlechty's writings for a detailed description of the WOW framework and standards, but these are the common classroom standards we use in discussing the *way we do business* in all classrooms of our school. Other schools may have different classroom standards, but whatever specific standards are in place, it is important that teachers share a common language about teaching and learning expectations within the school. Furthermore, disciplined conversations should occur between and among individuals and groups within the school centered on learning and continuous improvement. For our school to move from talk to action, we must establish a common language about schooling and ensure that we regularly use this language in discussing where we are in terms of meeting our classroom standards.

Although it is important that teachers within the school share a common language about teaching and learning, it is equally important that we develop a common language for students to learn and use as they immerse themselves in their own education. In our school we have embraced the work of Marzano and Pickering (2005) who outline a program for building students' academic vocabulary. Teachers at our school created a list of 30 essential academic vocabulary words for each subject offered at every grade. We call these lists our *30 on the Wall* because they are displayed in a prominent place in every classroom of our school. Every teacher, student, and parent is aware of these content area vocabulary words and students, are expected to become intimately familiar with each word during the school year. These are words that students must learn to master the learning outcomes of each course. Teachers work together by department to create 30 such words at each grade level for every subject area. So, in a middle school with grades 6 to 8, each student should leave having mastered 90 academic content words relating to science, social studies, math, and language arts. Carried over to the 9 to 12 high school, each student learns an additional 120 academic vocabulary words for each core academic area during their high school career. Teachers at our school refer to these 30 on the Wall posters throughout the year, with many placing colored stickers of some sort next to a word each time it is taught in class. Students often remind teachers during a lesson that a word that has been mentioned is one of the words from their 30 on the Wall. We agree with Marzano and Pickering that "Teaching specific terms in a specific way is probably the strongest action a teacher can take to ensure that students have the academic background knowledge they need to understand the content they will encounter in school" (2005, p. 1).

In addition to creating lists of 30 core vocabulary words for every course offered at our school, we also developed what we call a *Universal 30,* which includes 30 verbs representing learning behaviors which students will most often engage in during their academic career at our school across grade levels and content areas. This list includes words such as *characterize, clarify, summarize, analyze, classify,* and *investigate* and informs students and parents what actions students will most often be engaged in as a student at our school. We publish the Universal 30 in our student handbook each year to promote the learning behaviors we want students to develop.

Creating, using, and promoting a common language about teaching and learning at our school is an essential way we build our school culture and let all stakeholders know about our work as well as how we go about conducting it.

Teacher Induction and Mentoring

Another important component of promoting our school's culture is our teacher induction program. When hiring new teachers and working with them throughout their first year at our school, we have two overall goals. First, of course, we want them to learn all about our school and how we currently do business. Yet, we also want them to know that we hired them because we want to gain their insights for improving the way we currently do business. We spend a great deal of time—beginning at the interview stage of the hiring process—establishing our expectations for teachers at our school. One of these expectations is that even as new teachers we expect them to come right in and make a difference. We let them know that there is no pecking order at our school and that all ideas are evaluated on their merit rather than on the seniority of the person proffering the idea. We reiterate our belief that teachers new to our school are encouraged to offer suggestions for change during new teacher orientation and during induction sessions held throughout the year. As we recognize teachers for accomplishments each week at our school, we often recognize first-year teachers who have done something remarkable in terms of our school culture. At times this occurs when a new teacher steps in and behaves in a way that is aligned with our current practices and promotes the existing culture. At other times, however, we recognize new teachers who have come in and changed our school's culture for the better. The induction process at our school begins during the interview and is an ongoing process which we use to communicate *and improve* our school's culture.

As important as it is to welcome new teachers to the school by mentoring them, sharing stories with them, and encouraging them to make their voices heard, it is also important that we have an *induction* of sorts for our new students. At our schools, we do this for students rising up to middle school from elementary school or for eighth-grade students matriculating to the high school. We plan a number of transition activities so that students are aware of our school culture as they prepare to enroll. We also make it a point to *induct* students who move into our school from another school during the year or over the summer. Just as we assign mentor teachers to support and lead new teachers, we also assign students who serve as peer leaders to mentor any student who moves into our school district. As with our teacher mentor program, our student peer leaders attempt to educate new students in the various ways we do business, yet they also let new students know that their ideas are welcome. We have *stolen* many great ideas from both students and teachers who joined our ranks after teaching or learning at another school and shared ideas that were in place and successful at their previous schools.

Core Components

In reviewing the preceding list of ideas suggesting ways the school principal fulfills the leadership responsibility of *culture,* we determined that they fall into one or more of the following five categories, which seem to succinctly encapsulate what we see as the core components of this leadership responsibility:

Cornerstone #8: Culture Building
1. Regard and Renew: Culture-building principals honor people, history, systems, traditions, practices, and skills. They build on the present in an effort to improve the future.
2. Build Collaboration: Culture-building principals compel shared learning, teaching, growing, and refining by creating time, structures, and the capacity to connect. They model and celebrate cohesion.
3. Set Standards: Culture-building principals establish common language, work, and expectations to clarify shared goals and deepen understanding of purpose. They create a framework to inform and guide manners, decisions, and plans.
4. Generate Energy: Culture-building principals recognize, tap, and celebrate talent and leadership in all school stakeholders. They promote a sense of willingness, well-being, and shared accomplishment on a regular basis.

> ### 5. *Communicate With Care:*
> Culture-building principals foster open dialogue and honest conversation with all invested in the work. They value the importance of verbal and nonverbal exchanges and is first to model the way.

The culture-building leader plans for and responds to events during the day, which reveals this focus on culture and exhibits a relentless quest to instill this focus in other educators at the school. The following illustration provides a brief snapshot showing how the principal remains highly focused on clear, consistent, and effective communication within the school as she moves throughout her day.

A Glimpse of the Culture-Building Principal

"Today is one of my favorite days of the year," writes Natalie Parker with calm reflection. "Final exams are the culmination of our work, play, passion, tears, tenacity, laughs, and so much more. And as we have shaped student growth together, let us celebrate knowing that such growth is a natural and welcomed product of our interconnected core values, beliefs, and mission. Moreover, thank you for believing in, trusting, taking responsibility for, and caring for our students and each other every day. As a result I am confident today's exam outcomes will exceed our goal to increase overall final assessment scores by 5% from last semester. And similar to semesters past, I am assured that we will benefit from nearly 100% student and teacher attendance, thanks to the importance we have placed on presence throughout the year. Plus, today's *Final Formals* set a critical tone and model that final exams days are significant and worthy of formal dress by everyone at Cornerstone."

Next, Natalie reminds teachers of today's after school *Exam Cram* tutoring sessions. Students electing to exempt finals because of their 98/A or above class average are required to serve as tutors. Natalie proudly reports that the Exam Cram participants (mandatory for those students with a 75/C or below average) are down approximately 11% from last semester; and, in turn, student tutors are up by 14%.

Natalie asks everyone to administer the end-of-semester feedback surveys to all students during today's second- and fourth-block reviews. She reveals that the same feedback survey will be mailed to parents by the close of the week. Also, while students are taking their surveys, Natalie encourages every teacher to fill out a *state of the school* wellness survey designed by the TALENT (Teachers as Leaders Encouraging

---

New Thought) team in an effort to refine norms and better serve collaborative needs next semester.

Natalie also encourages Content Collaboration Teams to take part in their student assessment analysis, using Cornerstone Assessment Protocols, right away to refine assessments used during tomorrow's administration. Natalie also promotes a call home to parents if any student fails an exam before winter break and reminds teachers of Cornerstone's norm to return all parental calls and e-mails before leaving for winter break.

Lastly, Natalie invites everyone to attend today's brown bag lunch with her in the Professional Learning Community (PLC) to design specific job responsibilities for instructional coaches (ICs) serving each department next semester. She relays her excitement for this new leadership addition within each department and thanks everyone who volunteered to ensure greater, personalized teacher support and content-focused professional learning as a result. She concludes with an invitation to "assess and learn with passion!"

After printing the day's calendar; joining Harvey Nichols, head custodian, in their regular morning discussion concerning the day's events and needs; and greeting students traveling to first block, Natalie checks in with head counselor, Joanna Price, to see if she, along with the other counselors and Cornerstone's graduation coach, have finalized plans for a new student support group assisting with parental divorce or separation. Yet, after noting that Joanna is the on-call counselor today and meeting with a parent, Natalie decides to visit classrooms taking final exams.

As she walks down the hallway just outside the counseling suite, she is heartened to witness so many green cards welcoming classroom observations, even during final exams. In fact, Natalie notes no red cards discouraging classroom entrance in view. She also notices the SAT word of the day *commitment* posted prominently on each teacher's front board and reflects on the affect the common practice has made in building transcendent classroom knowledge. Natalie walks nearly every unpopulated hall to cheer on test takers with a thumbs up and a smile.

During transition to second block, Natalie briefly speaks to Robert Delatorre regarding his first-block exam, applauding his noteworthy academic efforts as of late, before concluding the conversation, mindful that he is not late to second block.

After escorting Robert to class, Natalie decides to join Robert's class as they prepare for tomorrow's second-block final exam. Natalie anticipates another technology-rich exam review from geometry teacher Aaron Bell and looks forward to seeing what this semester's review offers. Clearly thinking the same, a group of teachers traveling on their collaborative walk-through, armed with one of Cornerstone's five digital cameras, join Natalie as unobtrusively as possible. Welcomed, the walk-through group takes pictures of coteachers Aaron Bell and Kyle West harmoniously facilitating an interactive electronic review game using wireless voting instruments that were purchased through a grant Aaron and his Content Collaboration Team wrote and gained this year. The walk-through group plans to print and post pictures of both teachers on Cornerstone's *Collaboration Corral* wall with an adjoining paragraph detailing the collaboration observed and how Cornerstone's lesson design qualities, such as engagement and choice, were evident. After complimenting both teachers and students on their technology savvy and evidence of great learning this semester, Natalie departs with the walk-through group, holding the door for everyone exiting.

In the hallway, Natalie and the other teacher observers discuss what they witnessed and informally brainstorm ideas for incorporating the wireless voting instruments in a variety of ways, including PLC sessions. Each agrees that Aaron Bell and Kyle West are valuable members of the school who regularly share and train others in the latest technology, and they express excitement about heightened student engagement as a result.

Thanking the walk-through group for their efforts, Natalie visits a few other classroom reviews, grabs her lunch, and heads to the teacher lunchroom for today's *brown bag* discussion at the start of third block.

While there, Natalie greets the 36 teacher participants and thanks them for carving out precious time during final exams to take part. She relays her enthusiasm for the new ICs joining each department next semester and looks to the twelve ICs to first report out on the Clinical Coaching workshop they just completed through the National Staff Development Council. Moreover, she asks them to lead the discussion and cultivation of official IC job responsibilities with input from the others in attendance. Throughout, Natalie takes an active part in the discussion and is quick to quell any conversation that foresees their transitional work to the seven-period day as superordinate or an obstacle to proper installment of ICs next semester. Natalie assures that, especially with this group of quality teachers, anything can be accomplished. In addition, she compliments Jill Stevens for sharing copies of of the latest article in *The Journal of Staff Development* entitled "Coaches Help Teachers Collaborate," so informed decisions and plans can be made.

Thereafter, Natalie steps into her office to answer a few pressing e-mails, and gathers necessary paperwork for a Student Support Team meeting on Robert Delatorre she initiated herself. Next, Natalie makes the afternoon announcements including the encouragement noting that "the best predictor of future behavior is past behavior." As a result, Natalie assures that tomorrow will bring 100% faculty attendance, nearly perfect student attendance, and optimal success on remaining final exams, just like today. In conclusion, she invites every Cornerstone teacher and student to "extend your learning, yourself, and your heart."

Core Reflections

Consider the ideal *culture-building* actions of Principal Parker and use the space provided to jot down examples of each core component found within this glimpse. Next, reflect on your own culture-building leadership actions and include personal notes affirming your strengths and areas of needed growth.

Cornerstone #8: Culture Building

1. **Regard and Renew:**

2. **Build Collaboration:**

3. **Set Standards:**

4. **Generate Energy:**

5. **Communicate with Care:**

Personal Notes:

10

Soliciting Input to Achieve Output

Cornerstone #9:
The school principal fulfills the responsibility of input by ensuring that all teachers have a voice in running the school, actively involving teachers in the design, and implementation of important decisions and policies.

The final of nine leadership responsibilities identified by Marzano, Waters, and McNulty (2005), which fall directly under the purview of the school principal and ultimately relate to student achievement, is one the authors call, *input*. Although we have focused throughout this book on the nine leadership responsibilities that must be executed first and foremost by the school principal, it is important to note the authors' emphasis that the other 12 leadership responsibilities must be shared with school leadership teams, allowing input from all teachers and inviting key school leaders to assist the principal to promote student achievement. Of course, making the commitment to actively solicit input from teachers when making key decisions that affect the school must originate with the school principal; the principal must genuinely *want* input or any efforts will prove counterproductive. In recent years nearly all schools and organizations have adopted leadership models that encourage—to varying extents—shared decision making. According to Malvetti (1995), principals seek input when making decisions for several reasons, such as more and better ideas for school improvement; increased commitment to program/policy implementation; enhanced communication throughout the school community; higher levels of satisfaction for teachers and other stakeholders; and, most importantly, more powerful learning for students. Pojidaeff (1995) suggests that leaders invite participation in the management of the organization so that employees can use their intrinsic motivation to learn, achieve, gain esteem, look for better ways of doing things, and ultimately improve productivity and maintain consistently high quality and service. These reasons for soliciting *input* from those within the organization relate in some way to the goal that we wish to increase our *output*—in our case, the performance and commitment of our teachers, whose own level of success relates directly to our students' success.

To receive input from teachers within the school, the principal must then determine what type of decision-making structures to put in place. In previous chapters of this book, we have discussed school leadership teams, local school councils, parent-teacher organizations, student advisory councils, teacher advisory councils, professional learning communities, grade-level teams, and academic department teams. Each of these structures involves teachers or other stakeholders providing input to the principal. In this chapter our primary focus centers on gaining input from teachers, rather than other stakeholders. Our teachers, of course, are the people who have the greatest influence on student learning. As a result, they should be actively involved in decisions that affect their ability to perform their best in the classroom. To increase teacher effectiveness, teachers must believe that their behavior can affect the learning of their students. They must also believe that they have the power to make decisions that can affect their role as well as student performance (Enderlin-Lampe, 1995).

In creating structures aimed at soliciting teacher input, principals must foster effective teamwork, organizing teachers into groups that work with a focus on quality input. Malvetti (1995) states that all such teams should address six core questions regarding how they operate:

1. Purpose: What are the goals of the team? What are the desired outcomes? What is the scope of the team?

2. Players: Who are the members of the team and what are their roles?

3. Responsibility: What is the team's authority? How are they accountable and how will their effectiveness be evaluated?

4. Logistics: When, where, and how often will the team meet?

5. Operations: How will the team establish ground rules, develop agendas, and assign tasks?

6. Connections: How will the team's work connect with other teams or the school as a whole? How does the team communicate with the rest of the school regarding its progress, input, recommendations, and decisions?

Strong principals not only desire input from teachers, they actively solicit it and put into place structures for gaining input in a way that is purposeful, that is, in a way that is focused on learning and focused on results.

In analyzing 16 quantitative research studies examining 669 schools related to this school leadership theme, Marzano and coworkers (2005) found an overall correlation of 0.25 between the leadership responsibility of *input* and student academic achievement. *Knowing* that effectively gaining input from teachers may relate to student achievement, strong school principals set about *doing* those things that promote an atmosphere in which teachers are expected to provide input into all aspects of the school. In schools where principals actively seek teacher input, both teacher and student output is maximized. Principals who effectively fulfill the responsibility of *input* do so in a variety of ways. Following are just a few ways that principals can fulfill this responsibility as outlined in *School Leadership that Works* (Marzano, et al., 2005). These suggestions are described in some detail and then followed by a brief list of five thoughts summarizing our experiences in this critical area.

Input: Points to Ponder

School Leadership Teams

In previous chapters we have described several structural components in place at our schools that, in turn, promote a culture of shared decision making at all levels. Two of our most powerful structures for gaining input from teachers are our biweekly School Leadership Team (SLT) meetings and our weekly Professional Learning Community (PLC) meetings. The SLT in place at our school is comprised of 15 of our school's most respected teacher leaders representing all academic areas as well as school administrators. We meet for 90 minutes every other Thursday morning before school, dedicating 60 minutes to teaching and learning issues and 30 minutes to operational issues or concerns shared by any staff member. The members who comprise the committee are the key to the team's success. Leadership team members must be individuals who truly are the leaders in their area of the school. They cannot be selected based on their position alone or their length of tenure at our school; instead, they must be chosen because they are the teachers who their colleagues respect *and follow*. We have a representative body, which means that each individual on the SLT reports back to a team of teachers; but if we do not have a counselor on staff who is a true school leader, it may mean that an academic area teacher represents the counseling department at SLT meetings. As we mentioned in Chapter 5 when discussing *situational awareness*, we have a system in place for devoting the final 30 minutes of each SLT meeting to addressing concerns, suggestions, ideas, or problems submitted by teachers on one of our *White Cards*. Teachers turn these in to their SLT representative and the team discusses each until we reach consensus. Afterward, the SLT member most directly involved in the issue writes a response to the individual who submitted it, letting them know what was discussed, the consensus of the SLT, and thoughts regarding next steps, if any.

Most of the time at each SLT meeting is devoted to teaching and learning, rather than operations issues. Although we certainly discuss any issue pertaining to instruction, professional learning, curriculum, or assessment that arises during the school year, we also study a year-long theme during this time. One year we spent most of this time learning about the purpose and structure of PLCs. The following year we implemented our PLC format for conducting our core business on a school-wide basis. Another year we focused on assessment practices throughout the year, asking each team member to take the lead one week in sharing best assessment practices currently used within their department. Still another year, we focused on the slogan "Failure is Not an Option" examining the writing of Alan Blankstein and the subsequent video series related to this theme (2004). Our work with the SLT during that year centered on brainstorming strategies to ensure that all students turned in all assignments, decrease the failure rate, and design a series of intervention strategies for struggling students. In *School Leadership that Works*, the authors provide several factors that school leadership teams might identify as the *right work* for them to undertake over the course of a school year. At the school level, they identify five broad categories and 18 possible action steps, framed as questions that begin, "Is the next best thing to do in our school to . . ." (Marzano, et al., 2005, p. 110). School principals must plan for the work that SLTs will do throughout a school year and provide a focus for the input they seek from teacher leaders as well as the work in which they will engage. This list of questions targets a number of possible areas of focus for principals at any level who wish to gain teacher input regarding how to move the school forward. When choosing the *right work* to identify from such a list, principals must ask SLT members for input regarding the extent to which the school already engages in the behavior described, the extent to which student achievement will increase if the school changes its behavior, and how much effort it will take to change current practices relating to the issue. By having a year-long focus for this important block of time, team members become more focused on our purpose. They become more effective at communicating the work of the SLT to their respective teams and providing input they receive back to the SLT.

Input Through Professional Collaboration

Our PLC teams serve as our second major structure for soliciting teacher input into key issues facing our school. As stated previously, the key questions for which we are seeking input through our PLCs center on what we want students to learn, how we will know if they have learned it, and how we will respond when students do not learn or have already mastered the intended learning outcomes. The structure we have in place for soliciting and monitoring input through PLCs is in place as we begin each school year. PLC groups meet weekly either in small groups (teachers who teach the same subject at the same grade level, e.g., eighth-grade science teachers) or large groups (teachers in the entire department, e.g., all social studies teachers, grades 9–12). As teachers meet in these groups each week, administrators sit in as active participants and listeners, trying to gain insights into the core issues facing each academic area of the school. After each PLC meeting, a member of the group e-mails a *PLC Feedback Sheet* to the administrator assigned to that department. This feedback sheet is extremely simple; our goal is simply to keep in weekly contact with each PLC group to gain input and monitor progress toward stated goals relating to student achievement. Our intent is that completing the form take no more than a few minutes each week. The last question on our form solicits teacher input by asking teachers to pose any concerns or questions they have for school administrators. A sample of the form we currently use is provided on the following page.

Principals must plan for gaining input from teachers by providing structures in which teachers meet in teams to examine in a focused, purposeful way issues facing the school that ultimately affect student achievement. Although we have several such structures in place, the two overarching ways we gain regular and focused feedback from teachers is through our SLT, which works on school-wide issues, and our PLCs, which address topics related to specific academic areas.

An Open Door Policy

Many principals boast of having an *open door* policy so that teachers can drop in at any time to discuss an issue germane to the running of the school or simply to chat. Although we are rarely in our offices during the school day, we do try to foster an open door attitude within our staff, inviting them to approach us with any concern, idea, problem, or solution they might have regarding our school. During my first year as principal, I was surprised to note very few teachers ever dropped by my office during, before, or after school to talk about our school or just to visit. As a way to increase traffic by the principal's office, we placed a popcorn machine outside the office door and made several batches throughout the day, inviting teachers to stop by anytime for free popcorn. This had an immediate influence on a number of levels as teachers began coming by regularly. As they did, they almost always stepped into my office to see if I was there and to say hello. On several occasions, this prompted teachers to sit and discuss ideas they had for improving our school in some way. Although principals may not want to do this every day, we suggest doing something similar every Friday and making it a point to spend more time in the office on Fridays. If a popcorn machine is unavailable, principals might consider placing candy, pretzels, or bottled water outside their door as a way to thank teachers for a productive week and welcome them to provide direct, *drive-by* input.

The School Budget

Another important aspect of our school operations for which we seek teacher input is our school budget. Like principals at most schools, we do not have direct control over a great percentage of the school budget. However, each year our school is allotted a certain amount of money from the district for instructional purposes and professional learning, which we use at our own discretion. For our discretionary instructional funds, we ask each academic department to send a representative to a budget meeting in the spring to dedicate available dollars for the following school year. This process has been in pace for several years, so representatives now work cooperatively to fairly allocate all monies. Some years the science department may need additional money for lab equipment, whereas other years the math department may need a bigger slice of the pie to supplement a new textbook series. The fine arts department always has a lengthy wish list of budget items that will enrich the choral, drama, art, and band programs. Typically, department representatives share their current situations with the assembled group and make their cases for future needs, suggesting specific dollar amounts they are requesting. After representatives state their cases, as a group we begin examining how much we are over our budget at this point, after totaling all initial requests. Each team member then begins offering to shave off a certain amount of money from the original budget request to help a colleague in another department who may have greater needs for the following year. Working together, we come to a fairly quick and fair budget solution. By working in this manner—instead of simply dividing the money equally or having the principal determine the amount each department receives annually—we allow teachers to decide how our school's money should be spent. We regularly suggest that our classroom teachers make a difference in terms of student achievement. By allowing teachers to determine how these instructional funds are spent, we are honoring this belief and sending teachers the message that we value their input.

Team Feedback Sheet

Team: _____ Date: _____

Team SMART Goal(s): _____

_____

_____

_____

_____

_____

_____

Team Members Present: _____

_____

_____

_____

_____

_____

Team Members Absent (include reason for absence): _____

_____

_____

_____

_____

_____

_____

Meeting Topics/Products/Outcomes: _____

_____

_____

_____

_____

_____

Questions/Concerns from Team: _____

_____

_____

_____

_____

_____

Our school district also allocates each school in the system a certain amount of professional development money each year to use however best meets the needs of the local school community. Here again, we ask teachers for input on how this money should be spent. Although we keep some money in reserve for school-wide staff development, we divide the remaining amount between our PLC teams to spend in a way that best meets their professional growth goals. Some groups use this money for substitute teacher coverage so they can attend a conference, whereas others use the money for professional books and resources to help them learn new strategies. Still others have used this money to hire an expert in their subject area to speak with their group and share methods for differentiating instruction or working to improve writing skills. Some PLC Small Groups have even used this money to enroll in college courses to add a gifted endorsement to their teaching certificate during the school year. The amount of money we receive from our district to spend for professional growth and instructional resources is not vast, yet it is significant enough to make a difference. We feel that teachers should have a majority say in how these funds are expended for two reasons:

1. Typically, they are more aware than we are about their needs and what is available that would best fulfill these needs.

2. Teachers who have a voice in how these funds are spent tend to become more invested in the entire process and more committed to following through on professional growth goals.

Professional Learning

In addition to asking teachers for input in terms of how to spend a portion of monies available in our professional development budget, we also ask for their input in terms of our school wide professional growth plan. This is another process that begins near the end of the school year as we plan for the upcoming one. In asking teachers to help plan our professional learning activities for the new year, we ask only that they base their decisions on an area where the data indicates the school needs improvement. Over the years we have decided as an entire faculty to dedicate our school-wide professional learning to a variety of topics, including assessment, inclusion, strategies for working with ESOL students, writing across the curriculum, reading in the content areas, and building academic vocabulary. After deciding on our primary improvement target area, we then ask teachers to help us plan the activities in which we will engage as well as the resources needed to accomplish the intended learning objectives. As with budget issues, teachers who have a say in deciding what they will learn and how they will learn it are much more likely to become invested in actually learning it.

Another way teachers provide input at our school is by redelivering information learned at conferences they attend or through graduate or endorsement programs in which they are enrolled. In the case of the former, we always ask teachers to report to the administration after attending a conference regarding the value of what they learned. After listening carefully, we ask them if they feel that the learning gained is worth sharing with the entire staff. If so, which is almost always the case, we arrange for teachers to present a mini-session of the conference at a faculty meeting, during planning period meetings, or after school as an optional learning opportunity for teachers who might be most interested in the topic. In the case of the latter, although we certainly do not require teachers who have enrolled—on their own initiative—in graduate school or other programs of study to share what they are learning through their coursework, we always invite them to do so. Typically, teachers enrolled in such programs are among our best and are excited about what they are learning. Our hope is that this excitement infects others, making them curious about some aspect of their craft. Friedman (2006) suggests that no one works harder than a curious kid. We tend to agree and would add that a similar trend holds true for teachers: Those who are curious about how best to teach their students are likely to work the hardest at ensuring that students learn. There are many times throughout the year when we, as administrators, speak to teachers directly about teaching and learning at our school. Although we value these opportunities and feel we have much to offer our teachers, we also know that they enjoy learning from each other just as much, if not more.

Typically when we think of teachers offering input to others on the staff, we think of settings such as faculty meetings, at which teachers with a special expertise or interest related to teaching share what they know with their colleagues. As mentioned earlier, we often ask teachers to do just that. However, our whole-group faculty meeting time is limited; and when we do meet together, we often have a full slate of important agenda items to discuss, making it challenging to find the time for every teacher to share all the things they would like to present. One way we allow for additional opportunities for collegial and collaborative sharing is through our weekly Friday Focus writings. In Chapter 8 we described our system for creating and sharing these weekly writings dedicated to presenting information about a specific area of our profession. As principal, I look forward to writing these weekly memos myself, sharing with the entire school my passions related to teaching and learning. Yet, I am just as excited when a teacher at our school writes a Friday Focus. Almost every week, some teacher at our school approaches me and shares an idea they have for improving our school or an insight they have gleaned through experience that has improved their teaching. Oftentimes, the idea is so intriguing that I ask the teacher to share it with the entire staff through the Friday Focus format. Teachers seem to enjoy writing their thoughts about what they have learned and what they believe in and sharing this with their colleagues. Teachers who have authored Friday Focus memos always tell me how surprised they are by the amount and quality of feedback they receive from others on staff who read the weekly Friday Focus.

Hiring New Teachers

An important example of gaining input from our teachers occurs when we hire new teachers at our school. Although we always make it clear that the principal has the final say in who is hired and who is not, we never interview candidates without including teachers in the process. If we need to hire a math teacher, we always include as part of the interviewing team one or two teachers from the math department and teachers from the grade level at which the new teacher would be working. When we need to hire a new assistant principal, we include several teachers from the school leadership team on the interviewing panel. During these interviews teachers serving on the committee are encouraged to write and pose any question they wish to have answered. Often, teachers at our school devise questions superior to our own. After we interview a candidate for any position at our school, we always spend time going around the table comparing notes on each person interviewed before informally ranking our preferences. Although it is important that the principal make the final decision when hiring, our experience has been that we nearly always arrive at the same decision as the teachers who participate in this process. Inviting teachers to help interview and select candidates for teaching and administrative openings sends a clear message to teachers that their input is important.

Sharing Our Work

One final and simple way we gain teacher input is through posting information on a large bulletin board in our school's teacher workroom. On this wall teachers post a variety of material for others to read and examine. We ask all PLC Small Groups at our school to post their weekly feedback sheets so that all in the school can follow the progress of each academic team. Teachers display student work samples they have designed and test data from classroom assessments. At times, teachers simply share positive comments about a colleague they observed teaching or a math problem of the week they are using with their class. We post the school improvement plan on this bulletin board and ask teachers to add, change, delete, or edit items on the plan throughout the first half of the year, while we are still working to solidify our goals, our action steps, and the evidence we will collect to measure our success. Teachers also post articles they have read in professional journals, with a short note letting others know the merits of the article. Each year, teachers use this bulletin board as a way to share their own ideas and learn from their colleagues.

Core Components

In reviewing the preceding list of ideas suggesting ways the school principal fulfills the leadership responsibility of *input*, we determined that they fall into one or more of the following five categories, which seem to succinctly encapsulate what we see as the core components of this leadership responsibility:

Cornerstone #9: Input
1. *Involve Teachers:*   Input-focused principals genuinely value and recognize the importance of collaborating with all teachers. They ensure that teachers participate in all aspects of the school's functioning, including decision and policy making.
2. *Create Structures:*   Input-focused principals develop safe and focused teamwork opportunities for teachers to volley ideas, share learning, offer direction, and guide next steps for the good of students, the school, and each other.
3. *Solicit Feedback:*   Input-focused principals actively seek contributions from teachers in an effort to enhance their performance and commitment. They invite responses and divergent perspectives through formal and informal means.
4. *Strive for Consensus:*   Input-focused principals are sensitive to faculty needs and desires. They make sure teachers are empowered change agents who have a valued say and influence decision making on a regular basis.
5. *Reflect and Refine:*   Input-focused principals readily act on feedback from teachers. They honor their participatory investment by enacting changes and honing work for the betterment of student achievement and school improvement.

The input-focused leader plans for and responds to events during the day, which reveal this focus on input and exhibit a relentless quest to instill this focus in other educators at the school. The following illustration provides a brief snapshot of ways the principal remains highly focused on clear, consistent, and effective communication within the school as she moves throughout her day.

A Glimpse of the Input-Focused Principal

"Thank you," writes Natalie, "for the invaluable, meaningful feedback you provided these past few days through our departmental Articulation meetings, wellness surveys, walk-throughs, and Content Collaboration Team meetings and for proving James Surowiecki's research theory in his book *The Wisdom of Crowds* (2004) to be true. Just as Surowiecki suggests, leadership decision making is more accurate and less risky when entrusted to a diverse group rather than an individual. Specifically, as a result of your feedback, the Leadership Team and I will examine the following suggestions:

1. study and determine ways to best balance assessment and grading load, especially essays, in light of next year's seven-period day;

2. study and determine ways to best implement science labs in 50 minutes as opposed to 90 minutes and/or look at scheduling options that allow for lab courses adjoining selected science courses;

3. look into purchasing an online grading assessment tool to provide immediate feedback and ease formative grading load;

4. allow for a *70/30 Rule* to govern our PLC, 70% commonly directed focus and 30% individual team-directed focus based on each Content Collaboration Team's needs;

5. and lastly, purchase two more sets of wireless voting instruments so more students have access to this engaging technology each day.

After the Leadership Team provides input on these five suggestions today, we will provide you with implementation drafts for your consideration, insights, and vote by consensus before we move forward on any/all. And I look forward to collaborating alongside you tomorrow during our *Purposeful Postplanning* session from 8 to 11 a.m. in our PLC. In addition to these topics, we will also consider second-semester professional learning plans brought forth from our Standards Team, which meets today during third block."

Natalie also reminds teachers of tonight's holiday party and reveals that, because of subtle hints and not-so-subtle requests, she made an abundance of her popular peppermint candy bark and welcomes anyone interested to come by and enjoy some available in her office throughout the day. She adds that as a caveat to partaking, one must complete a *Valued View* card providing comments, suggestions, or feedback on any aspect of the school's functioning. She thanks, in advance, everyone willing to provide their good thinking for the betterment of Cornerstone, students, and each other. She concludes with an invitation to "assess and learn with passion!"

After printing the day's calendar, Natalie joins the Leadership Team, comprised of learning leaders representing each discipline, to take part in review and shared decision making regarding the five worthy suggestions brought forth from colleagues, other teams, and surveys. Before the team dives into the first topic on the agenda, Natalie reviews the protocol of consensus (when all points of view have been heard, and the will of the group is evident—even to those that most oppose it) used when deciding on whether the topic at hand is significant and meritorious enough to move forward to whole-faculty decision making, also by consensus. As a result, Natalie and the Leadership Team effectively examine and apply value to each review item so that only those worthy move to the next level of shared governance. Using the protocol, the team has time to offer creative, budget-friendly modifications to the original suggestions, which allow for more to become viable possibilities.

Thanking the Leadership Team for their serious investment in school improvement at the conclusion of the meeting, Natalie joins Stephanie Walker, on duty in the commons area before school. While there, the two discuss final exams and Stephanie relays her pleasure with the faculty's decision to move the last final exam to fourth block this semester. Agreeing, Natalie listens to Stephanie share concerns about balancing final exams on the forthcoming seven-period day. Stephanie feels strongly that students will need more than the usual 2-day allotment, which would call for students taking upward of four exams in one day. Natalie concurs, and assures that she will take this concern to their Leadership Team. In turn, Natalie asks Stephanie to create a few possible exam schedule options to share. Stephanie thanks Natalie and invites her to witness the student exit interviews she is conducting with her first-block students; they are modeled after the exit interviews seeking appraisal and feedback to guide improvement that Natalie conducts with teachers exiting Cornerstone. Excited, Natalie agrees to visit after the morning transition to class concludes.

Attending Stephanie's first-block class, Natalie is pleased that senior Rachel Riles is participating in her exit interview so Natalie can gain an update on her progress and growth. After listening to Rachel discuss her evidence of learning, detailing her comfort and success completing her writing portfolio, self-assessments, and subsequent gain in test scores, Natalie is heartened by Rachel's ability to articulate her learning and is pleased to remind Rachel that as a result a senior class ring, at Natalie's expense, awaits her choosing. Moreover, Natalie learns that their semester's *Assessment for Learning* focus in PLCs has had a positive affect on Stephanie's instruction and many other teachers she has observed as triangulation of learning evidence (conversations, observations, products) abounds.

After transitioning to second block, Natalie enters her office to find many completed Valued View cards. Reading each one carefully and pausing at one asking for Cornerstone's policy on assigning the grade of zero, Natalie collects them along with a few blank cards and posts them in the nearby teacher lunchroom on their discussion board. Commonly, teachers readily read and offer added points of view below each one on the adjacent blank cards inviting further comment. Most often, lunch discussion is an outgrowth of the topics brought forth by the Valued View cards; and if not, when Natalie joins the lunch table, she uses the topics as a springboard for conversation and feedback.

Reserving the one card asking for a grading policy, Natalie walks every hall of Cornerstone monitoring levels of quiet, frequency of student movement in the hallway, and testing atmosphere in classrooms as she intently observes for the remainder of second block.

Thereafter, she joins the Standards Team in the Professional Learning Center for their bimonthly assessment and planning meeting regarding Cornerstone's professional learning. To start, Natalie shares the Valued View card asking whether Cornerstone has an official grading policy when it comes to assigning zeroes. And even though nothing official is in writing, a collective understanding, as a direct result of their *Assessment for Learning* study, has lead nearly every teacher to ensure work completion, not allowing students to opt out of assigned work. Thus, this Valued View generates discussion and Natalie asks for everyone's input regarding the creation of a grading policy. After considered conversation and vote by consensus, the Standards Team decides to continue the *Assessment for Learning* study because it naturally provides foundational instructional/assessment practices that best guide decisions necessary when addressing homework, recovery, and pacing in PLCs. Also, the team feels the potential grading policy is worthy of a whole-faculty vote by consensus, but all feel that such a policy should not be enacted until the start of next school year because time to collaborate on and calibrate is necessary beforehand. Fully agreeing, Natalie thanks the Standards Team for their significant involvement, and "looks forwards to the meaningful professional learning ahead" as a result.

After observing fourth-block halls and classrooms during final exams, Natalie stops by her office to find many more Valued View cards. In her afternoon announcements she praises teachers' "complementary teamwork this semester because their ever-present passion for learning, investment in student achievement, and responsiveness to change has ensured student learning and assured final exam success." Moreover, Natalie encourages each Cornerstone teacher and student to "extend your learning, yourself, and your heart" during the winter break just as Natalie has observed them doing every day throughout the semester just completed.

Core Reflections

Consider the ideal *input-focused* actions of Principal Parker and use the space provided to jot down examples of each core component found within this glimpse. Next, reflect on your own input-focused leadership actions and include personal notes affirming your strengths and areas of needed growth.

Cornerstone #9: Input

1.   Involve Teachers:

2.   Create Structures:

3.   Solicit Feedback:

4.   Strive for Consens us:

5.   Reflect and Refine:

Personal Notes:

11

Schools That Learn

"Why is it that at the end of so many books and seminars, leaders report being enlightened and wiser, but not much happens in their organizations?" (Pfeffer and Sutton, 2000, p. 4). After reading *School Leadership that Works* (Marzano, Waters, and McNulty, 2005), we felt enlightened and wiser about what we, as school leaders, can and should do to optimize the performance of students and teachers. We also felt motivated to turn this knowledge into action. Our intent in this book is to extend the findings discovered by Marzano, Waters, and McNulty and provide practical applications for principals truly interested in fulfilling key leadership responsibilities positively correlated to student achievement. When we first read this powerful book on school leadership, we immediately realized that the authors had thoroughly scrutinized what most interested us about school leadership—how it affects student achievement—and identified the actions leaders must perform every day to make a difference in the lives of our most precious assets: our children. We decided to reflect on what we were currently doing and what we could do in the future to ensure that we were fulfilling the nine leadership responsibilities most directly controlled by the school principal:

1. Optimizer
2. Affirmation
3. Ideals/beliefs
4. Visibility
5. Situational awareness
6. Relationships
7. Communication
8. Culture
9. Input

In other words, we planned on turning the knowledge we gained into action. Every idea put forth in this book has been implemented and deemed a contributing factor to our school's success. Many of these practices are admittedly common sense ideas, which alone would not fulfill our unwavering goal of leadership with a purpose. Collectively, however, we feel that by planning for specific structures and systems that address these nine leadership responsibilities, we are turning knowledge into actions, which ultimately translate into greater teacher and student performance.

Our ultimate goal as school leaders is to establish and sustain a learning environment. It should thrive as the *purposeful learning community* described in Chapter 1 and, as Marzano and colleagues (2005) suggest, consist of four key components:

1. Collective efficacy
2. Development and use of all available assets
3. Goals that matter to all community members
4. Agreed-on processes

We believe that the most important of these four pillars is collective efficacy, the degree to which those in the organization believe they have the power to enhance the effectiveness of the organization and can make a difference in terms of student learning. *School Leadership that Works* (Marzano, et al. 2005) goes beyond *believing* that school leaders can make this difference, providing clear evidence that drives us toward *knowing* this is so. It remains the responsibility of school principals and other school leaders to purposefully act on this knowledge and identify and execute specific strategies for addressing each leadership responsibility examined in this book.

In this book we share many actions we have taken as school leaders that we believe specifically address these responsibilities. Many actions we describe in the preceding chapters stand as ways to address more than one of the nine responsibilities. Much of what we do to cultivate collegial and collaborative *relationships* is closely related to how we *communicate*. The actions we take to ensure that we fulfill the responsibility of *visibility* also help to make us more *situationally aware*. We suggest that principals begin the process of fulfilling these nine leadership responsibilities by listing all practices currently in place within their schools that address any of the responsibilities, including certain actions that apply to more than one category, as appropriate. Principals at all schools will likely identify many examples of how they are already leading in a way that touches on all areas. Next, we suggest that principals commit to creating a *list of five* for each of the nine domains. That is, refine the original list of actions to ensure that under each area of responsibility, principals have five actions that they currently practice or can carry out in the future, which serve the purpose of fulfilling each responsibility. Of course, we have offered many possible ideas within this book; but we realize that every school is unique, with different needs, strengths, personalities, demographics, sizes, facilities, grade configurations, budgets, goals, and dreams. Yet, with all these differences, we share a common, overarching goal: to enhance student learning. It has become commonplace in schools across the nation to talk of doing *whatever it takes* to ensure that students learn. Too often, these words are unaccompanied by actions and often, when actions are initiated, they are not done with purpose.

In acting on this knowledge and encouraging other school leaders to do the same, we have embraced four guiding principles. They compel us to move forward in initiating change and ensuring that we adopt practices that address the nine responsibilities and eliminate some that do not. Each principle has helped us move from *knowing* what to do *acting* on this knowledge. Focusing on these principles and the nine leadership responsibilities examined in this book should help school leaders create what we call *schools that learn*.

Clarifying the Core

The principal is the ultimate leader of the school. Regardless of how interested a principal is in soliciting input from others at the school and in the community when making decisions regarding the running of the school, at the end of the day the principal is responsible, directly or indirectly, for all that affects the school. No initiative can succeed without the support of the building principal. Conversely, with the principal's full and enthusiastic support, almost any initiative can be implemented; and with ongoing monitoring and evaluation most, if not all, succeed. We believe, therefore, that principals must share their core values with the entire staff at the outset of every school year. The issues facing school leaders are numerous and multifarious. No single leader can be an expert in, nor exhibit a true passion for, all these many issues. Conversely, each of us has an interest, expertise, and passion for certain aspects of education that propel us to act with passion and purpose. At the beginning of each school year, we meet to revisit what we call: *Clarifying our CORE Values*. For us, the C in *clarifying* represents collaboration; the other letters stand for communication, observation, relationships, and expectations. These are the core values we adhere to as school leaders, and we share these with our teachers every year. Our overarching goal is to instill and promote a culture of collaboration in our schools, and we emphasize the other four strands of our core values as we do so. Of course, others in our school possess their own individual core values. Many are passionate about specific areas of teaching and learning, classroom management, or assessment practices. We feel that it is vital to engage teachers in dialogue on the issue of our core educational values at the beginning of every school year. Within each school, teachers must know what their principals stand for, their non-negotiable core values. In addition, they must share their own beliefs and values. To lead our students to academic success, we must commit to shared core values and to sharing our particular areas of strength and passion with others in the school. Principals who lead schools that learn begin by clarifying core values.

Learning by Doing

Even principals who have served in that role for many years at the same school should begin the year by initiating a discussion of their own—and the school's—core values. Sharing our stories, our beliefs, and our commitments are vital to charting the course of actions that follow over the course of the school year. As important as this is, it is also important to act on these core values and commitments. This, perhaps, is the very essence of what we have discussed in this book: moving from knowledge of what effective school leaders do to acting on that knowledge. Too often, and for a variety of reasons, we remain stuck in the *knowing-talking* phase of improving our schools without ever advancing to the "knowing-acting" phase. At times, we wait for a strong consensus among the entire staff. At others, we resist because of limited resources or lingering doubts about the potential success of the proposed action. It is our fervent belief that school leaders must call those within their schools to action. Although it sounds paradoxical, we maintain that schools do not learn by knowing. Rather, they learn by doing. This does not mean that we try out every new idea that comes our way. To do so is to guarantee failure. However, it does mean that we set our course, guided by a firm foundation of shared values and goals, and choose to undertake actions that are designed to uphold these values and meet these goals. Our very best teachers risk failure regularly as they experiment with new ideas aimed at helping our students learn. School leaders must encourage this willingness to take risks to succeed. Every time we try something new at our school we are learning. On occasion, we learn what does not work; more often, we find that by doing, we learn what does work. We are no different in this regard than the students we teach. Although they need a sound knowledge base in all areas to succeed, if students never move beyond *learning about* the content to *performing the actions* related to the content, they will never truly learn. For educators, this same progression must occur. Principals who lead schools that learn, know that schools learn by doing.

Behaviors Before Beliefs

In schools, teachers take actions each day within their own classrooms as they work to improve learning for their students. Yet, it is also necessary that teachers act outside their individual classrooms in ways that support the school's values and help the school meet school-wide improvement goals. Our best teachers accept this responsibility, working in a collegial and collaborative manner to meet the needs of all students, while helping to maintain a positive school culture. In every school at which we have worked, we have also encountered teachers who are not intrinsically motivated to work in such a way. Although it is always preferable and more productive when teachers act willingly because they share the beliefs, values, and goals of the school, in instances when teachers do not subscribe to these beliefs, it is important for principals to focus instead on their behaviors. Ideally, teachers who change their *behaviors*, eventually change their *beliefs* in a way that aligns with those espoused by the rest of the school. In a worst-case scenario, resistant teachers cling to their own beliefs, yet still change their behaviors, which once again moves schools forward from knowing/believing to doing. Principals determined to implement positive changes in schools know that not all teachers believe in every school-based initiative. Strong principals move forward despite these resistant teachers and focus on changing behaviors, if not beliefs, of all teachers. If we change the behaviors of our mediocre, resistant teachers, we have still turned knowledge into action. Over time, many teachers adopt new beliefs after seeing first-hand, positive results from changing their behaviors. For most staff, we recommend focusing on beliefs first, then calling on teachers to behave in a way that upholds these beliefs. Yet, it is equally important to accept that not all teachers share in the beliefs of the majority. In such cases principals leading schools that learn focus on behaviors first, then beliefs.

Urgency Over Obstacles

Too often in education, moving from knowing what to do to actually doing it never occurs because too many stakeholders are overly vigilant in pointing out the numerous obstacles and pitfalls that face us each day. Our students are from economically disadvantaged families, the family structure in our society has broken down, we have too many students who are not fluent in English, our facilities are inadequate, our budgetary resources constrain us, our kids will not do homework, and No Child Left Behind has forced us all to teach to the test. These are but a few of the litany of obstacles that face educators throughout our nation. Although many of these problems are very real, there is an even more important reality: They are not going away. We must accept the challenges that face us, admitting that many are daunting, yet still move forward with a sense of urgency. Successful schools do not allow obstacles—no matter how imposing—to stand as an impediment to action. Successful school leaders do not dismiss these obstacles by suggesting they are not real or are insignificant. Instead, they acknowledge the problems as genuine yet insist that the school's mission compels it to act with a sense of urgency to accomplish its goals. We are here to make a difference and accomplish important work, not to explain why we cannot accomplish all that we would like. Strong principals who lead schools that learn understand that obstacles to success are real and must be addressed, yet instill a sense of urgency that commits all educators within the school to engage in actions aimed at overcoming obstacles.

For the school principal forced to deal with hundreds of issues each week that are not directly related to teaching and learning, it is easy to become distracted and lose sight of what is most important about the role of the principal: taking actions that result in higher levels of learning for all students. We acknowledge the meta-analysis conducted by Marzano and colleagues (2005) is the best tool available to inform the work of school leaders interested in aligning their practices to those identified as directly or indirectly relating to student academic achievement. Any school leader who reads this meta-analysis *knows* the leadership responsibilities that affect student achievement and that must be fulfilled by school leaders. We now call on principals and other school leaders armed with this knowledge to *act* in purposeful ways designed to create *schools that learn,* schools where students and teachers are engaged in thoughtful actions aimed at increasing student academic achievement.

References

Barth, R. S. (1990). *Improving schools from within: Teachers, parents, and principals can make the difference.* San Francisco: Jossey-Bass.

Barth, R. S. (2001). *Learning by heart.* San Francisco: Jossey-Bass.

Bell, L. (1992). *Managing teams in secondary schools.* London: Routledge.

Bernhardt, V. L. (1998). *Data analysis for continuous school improvement.* Larchmont, NY: Eye On Education.

Blankstein, A. M. (2004). *Failure is not an option: Six principles that guide student achievement in high-performing schools.* Thousand Oaks, CA: Corwin.

Blase, J. J., & Kirby, P. C. (2000). *Bringing out the best in teachers: What effective principals do.* Thousand Oaks, CA: Corwin.

Broh, B. (2002). Linking extracurricular programming to academic achievement: Who benefits and why? *Sociology of Education, 75*(1), 69–91.

Castle, T. D. (1986). *The relationship of extracurricular activity involvement to I.Q., academic achievement, attendance, and discipline referrals at a selected Midwestern high school.* Unpublished doctoral dissertation, Drake University, Des Moines, IA.

Clark, R. (2003). *The essential 55: An award-winning educator's rules for discovering the successful student in every child.* New York: Hyperion.

Collins, J. (2001). *Good to great: Why some companies make the leap . . . and others don't.* New York: Harper Collins.

Covey, S. R. (1989). *The 7 habits of highly effective people: Powerful lessons in personal change.* New York: Simon and Schuster.

Davies, A. (2000). Making classroom assessment work. Courtenay, BC: Classroom Connections.

Downey, C. J., Steffy, B. E., English, F. W., Frase, L. E., & Poston, W. K. (2004). *The three-minute classroom walk-through: Changing school supervisory practice one teacher at a time.* Thousand Oaks, CA: Sage.

DuFour, R., & Eaker, R. (1998). *Professional learning communities at work: Best practices for enhancing student achievement.* Alexandria, VA: Association for Supervision and Curriculum Development.

DuFour, R., DuFour, R., Eaker, R., & Karhanek, G. (2004). *Whatever it takes: How professional learning communities respond when kids don't learn.* Bloomington, IN: National Education Service.

Eccles, J. S., & Barber, B. L. (1999). Student council, volunteering, basketball, or marching band: What kind of extracurricular involvement matters? *Journal of Adolescent Research, 41*(1), 10–43.

Elbow, P. (1986). *Embracing contraries: Explorations in learning and teaching.* New York: Oxford University.

Elmore, R. (2000). *Building a new structure for school leadership.* New York: Albert Shanker Institute.

Enderlin-Lampe, S. (1995). Shared decision making in schools: Effect on teacher efficacy. *Education, 118*(1), 150–157.

Esquith, R. (2003). *There are no shortcuts: How an inner-city teacher—winner of the American Teacher Award—inspires his students and challenges us to rethink the way we educate our children.* New York: Pantheon.

Farber, S. (2004). *The radical leap: A personal lesson in extreme leadership.* Chicago: Dearborn.

Friedman, T. (2006). *The world is flat: A brief history of the twenty-first century.* New York: Farrar, Straus and Giroux.

Fullan, M. (2003). *The moral imperative of school leadership.* Thousand Oaks, CA: Corwin.

Fullan, M. G., & Hargreaves, A. (1992). *What's worth fighting for in your school?* Buckingham: Open University.

Goldring, L. M. (2002). The power of school culture. *Leadership, 32*(2), 32–35.

Goleman, D., Boyatzis, R. E., & McKee, A. (2002). *Primal leadership: Realizing the power of emotional intelligence.* Boston: Harvard Business School.

Kmetz, J. T., & Willower, D. J. (1982). Elementary school principals' work behavior. *The Educational Administration Quarterly, 4*, 62–78.

Kohn, A. (2006). *The homework myth: Why our kids get too much of a bad thing.* Cambridge, MA: De Capo.

Kouzes, J. M., & Posner, B. Z. (1987). *The leadership challenge: How to get extraordinary things done in organizations.* San Francisco: Jossey-Bass.

Little, J. W. (1981). *The power of organizational setting: School norms and staff development.* Washington, DC: National Institute of Education. (ERIC Document Reproduction Service No. ED221918)

Lundin, S. C., Paul, N., & Christensen, J. (2000). *FISH! A remarkable way to boost morale and improve results.* New York: Hyperion.

Malvetti, N. L. (1995). Shared decisions. *Thrust for Educational Leadership, 24*, 13–18.

Marzano, R. J. (2000). *Transforming classroom grading.* Alexandria, VA: Association for Supervision and Curriculum Development.

Marzano, R. J., & Pickering, D. J. (2005). *Building academic vocabulary: Teacher's manual.* Alexandria, VA: Association for Supervision and Curriculum Development.

Marzano, R. J., Pickering, D. J., & Pollock, J. E. (2001). *Classroom instruction that works: Research-based strategies for increasing student achievement.* Alexandria, VA: Association for Supervision and Curriculum Development.

Marzano, R. J., Marzano, J. S., & Pickering, D. J. (2003). *Classroom management that works: Research-based strategies for every teacher.* Alexandria, VA: Association for Supervision and Curriculum Development.

Marzano, R. J., Waters, T., & McNulty, B. A. (2005). *School leadership that works: From research to results.* Alexandria, VA: Association for Supervision and Curriculum Development.

McEwan, E. K. (2003). *7 steps to effective instructional leadership.* Thousand Oaks, CA: Corwin.

McNeal, R. (1995). High school extracurricular activities: Closed structures and stratifying patterns of participation. *The Journal of Educational Research, 91,* 183–191.

Mikkelsen, V. P., & Joyner, W. (1982). Organizational climate of elementary schools and reading achievement of sixth grade pupils. *Reading Improvement, 19,* 67–73.

Palmer, P. J. (1998). *The courage to teach: Exploring the inner landscape of a teacher's life.* San Francisco: Jossey-Bass.

Pfeffer, J., & Sutton, R. I. (2000). *The knowing-doing gap: How smart companies turn knowledge into action.* Boston: Harvard Business School.

Pickett, J. P., et al. (2000). *The American heritage dictionary of the English language* (4th ed.). Boston: Houghton Mifflin.

Pojidaeff, D. (1995). The core principles of participative management. *Journal for Quality and Participation, 18,* 44–50.

Reeves, D. B. (2006). *The learning leader: How to focus school improvement for better results.* Alexandria, VA: Association for Supervision and Curriculum Development.

Reeves, D. B. (2007). How do you change school culture? *Educational Leadership, 64,* 92–94.

Rice, G., & Taylor, G. (1985). *The peanut butter and jelly guide to teaching.* Vicksburg, MS: ETSI.

Robbins, P., & Alvy, H. B. (2004). *The new principal's fieldbook: Strategies for success.* Alexandria, VA: Association for Supervision and Curriculum Development.

Saphier, J. (2005). Effort-based ability. In R. DuFour, R. Eaker, & R. DuFour (Eds.), *On common ground* (pp. 85–113). Bloomington, IN: National Education Service.

Saphier, J., & King, M. (1985). Good seeds grow in strong cultures. *Educational Leadership, 42*(6), 67–74.

Schlechty, P. C. (2002). *Working on the work: An action plan for teachers, principals, and superintendents.* San Francisco: Jossey-Bass.

Schlechty, P. C. (2005, January). *The characteristics of schools operating as learning organizations.* Paper presented at the Principals' Academy, San Antonio, TX.

Schmoker, M. J. (2006). *Results now: How we can achieve unprecedented improvements in teaching and learning.* Alexandria, VA: Association for Supervision and Curriculum Development.

Senge, P. M. (1990). *The fifth discipline: The art and practice of the learning organization.* New York: Doubleday/Currency.

Silliker, S. A., & Quirk, J. T. (1997). The effect of extracurricular activity participation on the academic performance of male and female high school students. *School Counselor, 44,* 288–293.

Surowiecki, J. (2004). *The wisdom of crowds: Why the many are smarter than the few and how collective wisdom shapes business, economies, societies, and nations.* New York: Doubleday.

Wallace, M., & Huckman, L. (1999). *Senior management teams in primary schools.* London: Routledge.

Whitaker, T., Whitaker, B., & Lumpa, D. (2000). *Motivating and inspiring teachers: The educational leader's guide for building staff morale.* Larchmont, NY: Eye On Education.

Whitaker, T. (2003). *What great principals do differently: Fifteen things that matter most.* Larchmont, NY: Eye On Education.

Whitaker, T. (2004). *What great teachers do differently: Fourteen things that matter most.* Larchmont, NY: Eye On Education.

Zoul, J. (2006a). *Improving your school one week at a time: Building the foundation for professional teaching and learning.* Larchmont, NY: Eye On Education.

Zoul, J. J. (2006b). The role of interscholastic athletic participation and its relationship to educational outcomes at selected middle schools in the state of Georgia. Unpublished doctoral dissertation, The University of Alabama, Tuscaloosa, AL.